EASTERN ORTHODOXY COMPARED

Her Main Teachings and Significant Differences
with Roman Catholicism
and the Major Protestant Denominations

Rev. Fr. Constantine Mathews
Protopresbyter

Foreword by Archbishop Demetrios

Light & Life Publishing Company
Minneapolis, Minnesota

Light & Life Publishing Company
P.O. Box 26421
Minneapolis, MN 55426-0421

The icon on the cover is a copy of the one given by Ecumenical
Patriarch Athenagoras to Pope Paul VI at their historic meeting in
Jerusalem on January 5, 1964. The icon, created by the monk
Meletios of Mount Athos, depicts the two Apostles and brothers, Peter
and Andrew.

ISBN 1-933654-01-5

To my beloved wife, Presbytera Anna Mathews,
whose love of and dedication to the Orthodox faith is
an inspiration to all who know her.

AKNOWLEDGEMENTS

I must offer an acknowledgement and note of gratitude to my son, Nikiforos Mathews, who reviewed and edited this work with great patience. I also thank Fr. George Demopoulos, Fr. Nicholas Dasouras and Fr. Alkiviadis C. Calivas for their thoughtful review and comment.

ABOUT THE AUTHOR

The author, Fr. Constantine Mathews, is a graduate of the Kapodistriakon University of Athens, Greece, in 1969, and received his Master's Degree in Liturgical Studies from the University of Notre Dame in 1977. He has served as parish priest in Stamford, Connecticut, since 1978.

Foreword

Reverend and dear Fr. Constantine,

I would like to thank you for the book you produced entitled, Eastern Orthodoxy Compared: Her Main Teachings and Significant Differences with Roman Catholicism and the Major Protestant Denominations. We are hopeful that this book will serve as a helpful reference for our clergy, our faithful and for those seeking to learn more about our Orthodox Church and her faith.

The year 2005 has been designated by our Archdiocese as the Year of the Family. For this reason I am particularly pleased that you dedicate your book to a precious member of your family, namely Presbytera Anna, whose love and dedication to the Church, and to your family, are a symbol of devotion to your sacred ministry as a priest.

May the Lord continue to inspire you in your sacred diaconia and guide you in your personal work for the edification of the people and for the glory of His holy Name.

With paternal love and blessings,

+DEMETRIOS
Archbishop of America

TABLE OF CONTENTS

PROLOGUE

Faithful frequently ask me, "Father, are there really significant differences between the Christian faiths? After all, isn't there only one God?" While there is indeed one true God, unfortunately He is unknown to many.[1] This work discusses the significant differences between Eastern Orthodoxy and both Roman Catholicism and the major Protestant denominations. (The reader should keep in mind that this work is only a summary of differences regarding important and complex issues of faith.)

The Eastern Orthodox Church is a repository of Christian truths as received from Christ, His Apostles, the Apostolic Fathers who immediately followed the New Testament period, the other Fathers of the Church and the various regional and ecumenical councils, or meetings of bishops, of early Christianity. As such, the Eastern Orthodox Church has a great responsibility to inform its faithful—and all Christians—of the treasures that it has preserved unadulterated for twenty centuries.

---

[1] Acts 17:23. Unless otherwise indicated, all biblical quotations are from the Common Bible: The Revised Standard Version, 1973.

To understand the differences existing today between the East[2] and West, [3] one first must understand the historical developments that gave rise to or influenced these differences. From very early Christian times, the Church established by the Apostles was divided into five administrative districts, each with its own bishop: Rome, Byzantium (later known as Constantinople and today as Istanbul), Alexandria, Antioch and Jerusalem. The bishop of Rome was honored as the "first among equals," in deference to his position as bishop of the Roman Empire's capitol, yet the bishops, as successors to the Apostles, shared the same spiritual authority and prestige. In 330[4], Emperor Constantine transferred the seat of the Roman Empire to Byzantium and the honor bestowed upon the bishop of Rome was also bestowed upon the bishop of Byzantium (also known as the "Patriarch"). Shortly thereafter, in 393 A.D., Emperor Theodosius divided the Empire into two sections, the east, with Constantinople as its capital, and the west, with Rome as its capital. Nevertheless, the five administrative districts of the Church continued to operate independently and

---

[2] "Eastern Orthodox Church," "Eastern Church" and "East" are used interchangeably in this work.

[3] "Roman Catholic Church," "Western Church" and "West" are used interchangeably in this work.

[4] Unless otherwise noted, all dates in this work are "A.D."

democratically, without infringing upon one another's internal affairs. As a result, during the first eight centuries of Christianity, the Churches of the East and West were united by the common decisions of regional councils, as well as seven "ecumenical" councils, at which representatives from all geographic areas of the Christian world were present.[5] However, against a backdrop of political and jurisdictional disputes, East and West found themselves increasingly at odds.

The most significant dispute occurred in 858 A.D. with the election of Photius as Patriarch of Constantinople. The bishop of Rome (or "Pope")[6] Nicholas I, objected to Photius' election without his permission and refused to recognize him as Patriarch. The Pope voiced his objections openly, even sending a letter to the Emperor of Byzantium and, by so doing, interfered with the ecclesiastical affairs of another district. Increased distrust and discord ensued. Finally, in 1054, the differences between East and West came to a head.

---

[5] Note that many of the decisions of the twenty or so regional councils of the early Church were incorporated into the decisions of the seven Ecumenical Councils.

[6] "Pope" derives from the Greek word for father, "papas." Evidence suggests that by the fourth century the bishop of Rome was sometimes called "pope" and, by the eighth century, he was almost exclusively referred to as "the Pope."

At that time, representatives of Pope Leo IX traveled from Rome to Constantinople with letters demanding that the Patriarch of Constantinople, Michael Cerularios, submit to the primacy of the Pope, or Bishop of Rome. Upon Patriarch Cerularios' rejection of this demand, the papal representatives produced a previously-prepared document of anathema (essentially, excommunication) from Pope Leo IX, which they placed on the Holy Table of the cathedral of St. Sophia during the Divine Liturgy on July 15, 1054. In turn, Patriarch Cerularios organized a synod held in Constantinople on July 20, 1054, which anathematized those who sent and delivered the papal document.[7] This conflict, which formally separated the Eastern and Western Churches, came to be known as the "Great Schism."

Shortly after the Great Schism, during the Crusades, the Western Church again focused its attention on the Eastern Church. The initial purpose of the Crusades was to free the Holy Lands from the dominance and persecution of non-Christians. However, the long-standing legacy of the Crusades proved to be a cause for bitterness by Muslims against Christianity, and the weakening and ultimate destruction of the Byzantine Empire, the seat of the Ecumenical Patriarchate for Eastern Orthodoxy.

---

[7] Παπαδοπούλου, σ. 224-227.

The Crusaders may have worn large crosses on their chests, but they inflicted unspeakable destruction upon the Eastern Orthodox people of the Byzantine Empire. The fourth Crusade, led by the Venetians, severely depleted Byzantine military and financial power until, finally, Constantinople was sacked in 1204. The Emperor was deposed and replaced with Baldwin of Flanders and the Crusaders set about desecrating tombs and plundering churches, stealing holy relics (many of which were transported west, where they remain today) and carrying off whatever loot they could carry.

Almost immediately after the sack and subsequent occupation (which lasted until 1261) of Constantinople, Pope Innocent III installed his own Patriarch, Thomas Morosoni. A brutal persecution of Eastern Orthodox clergy ensued.[8] Moreover, each time the Crusaders captured a Byzantine city, a papal bishop was installed to impose the Pope's teachings on the area's Eastern Orthodox Christian population and to force the citizens to adopt Roman Catholic teachings in a coerced union under

---

[8] Παπαγιαννίδου, σ. 56.

[9] Shortly before the fall of Constantinople to the Ottomans, the Pope again tried unsuccessfully to impose a forced union between the Western and Eastern Churches at the Ferrara-Florence Council (1438-40).

the Pope.[9] As a result of the barbaric behavior of the Crusaders, which arguably was worse than that of even the Ottoman Turks in 1453, Constantinople was deserted by much of its population.

The Eastern Orthodox churches that came into "union" with the Roman Catholic Church following the sack of Constantinople came to be known as "Uniat" churches.[10] Rome generally permitted Uniat priests to marry, wear their Orthodox vestments, and perform the Liturgy in their own language and using Eastern rites.[11] Nevertheless, while the Uniat churches retained the traditional Eastern Orthodox liturgy and clerical dress, they acknowledged the supremacy of the Pope. Uniats often caused Orthodox communities to unite with the Roman Catholic Church by force.[12] A prominent example of this is the 1596 "Union of Brest," where, after much propaganda and a bitter struggle, the Polish Orthodox

---

[10] Some historians note that Uniat-type activity began as early as 885 A.D., before the Great Schism, when many churches were coerced into coming under the authority of Rome as a result of disputes over jurisdiction during the days of Cyril and Methodius and the conversion to Christianity of the Slavs and other Eastern European peoples. Certain Uniats are known today as "Eastern Rite Catholics" and "Greek Catholics."

[11] Στεφανίδου, p. 382.

[12] Παπαγιαννίδου, σ. 156.

Church submitted to the supremacy of the Pope.[13] Even as recently as 1955, "Pope Pius XII called upon the 'Uniat' Church to use its utmost to bring the Orthodox Churches to the 'fold.'"[14]

Nine-hundred and eleven years after the Great Schism, on December 7, 1965, the anathemas of 1054 were lifted by both churches, that of the Eastern Orthodox Church by Ecumenical Patriarch Athenagoras I and that of the Roman Catholic Church by Pope Paul VI. Nevertheless, neither the original points of contention, nor those that arose between the East and West in the centuries after the Great Schism, have been resolved.

---

[13] Ibid., p. 156. Great bitterness remains over this event, as was clearly evident during the 1996 anniversary of the event.

[14] Mastrantonis, *What is the Eastern Orthodox Church?*, p. 31.

PART ONE: A BRIEF INTRODUCTION TO EASTERN ORTHODOXY

There live in North and South America today approximately six million Christians who are neither Roman Catholic nor Protestant. They are members of the Eastern Orthodox Church. Many of them were transplanted to the Americas from Greece, Turkey, Russia, Yugoslavia, Romania, Bulgaria, Albania, Cyprus, Syria, Israel, Lebanon, Egypt and other lands of Eastern Europe and the Near East in which the ancient Orthodox Church has been—and remains—the dominant expression of Christianity for twenty centuries.

The Eastern Orthodox Church is comprised of several national churches of nearly identical dogma and practice of faith, which together account for more than 350 million followers worldwide. The Orthodox Church is not confined by geographic or ethnic boundaries, but embraces all people who desire to join a body of faithful united in an ancient form of worship traced to the early Church. The Eastern Orthodox Church prides itself on having maintained the beliefs and practices of the early Church, as passed on through tradition and as set forth in the decrees that resulted from the original regional and

1

ecumenical councils. As H.A. Hodges, an Anglican theologian, acknowledges:

> *I am speaking on the level of doctrine, and saying that the Orthodox Faith, that Faith to which the Orthodox Fathers bear witness and of which the Orthodox Church is the abiding custodian, is the Christian Faith in its true and essential form, to which we all aspire and by which we are all judged.[15]*

The Eastern Orthodox Church is a continuation of the early Church established by the Apostles, which in 381 was reaffirmed as "The One, Holy, Catholic and Apostolic Church" by the Second Ecumenical Council in Constantinople.[16] The Eastern Church is indeed "Apostolic," not only historically, but also in faith, discipline, the succession of the priesthood, the sacraments, tradition, practice and spirit.[17] There are two

---

[15] p. 47.

[16] The word "catholic" in this context does not refer to the Roman Catholic Church but, rather, means "pleres" (πλήρης), or full and complete in faith and practice, absolute in truth.

[17] The Eastern Orthodox Church has been criticized for its focus on early Church worship and for not "changing with the times." Yet, as Julius Tyciak, a German Roman Catholic theologian, explains in his book *Zwischen Morgenland und Abendland* (i.e., *Between East and West*):

2

sources of its teachings: (i) the books of the divinely
inspired New Testament, and (ii) the unwritten and orally
transmitted Apostolic teachings known as "Apostolic
Tradition." These sources, together with the dogmas and
teachings of the early Church through the Seventh
Ecumenical Council, known as "Ecclesiastical Tradition,"
comprise "Holy Tradition," the foundation of Orthodoxy.[18]
The Apostles and the Fathers, with the power of Christ and
the enlightenment of the Holy Spirit, nourished the true
faith, fought heresies, separated the canonical books from
the apocryphal,[19] formed the hierarchical Church
government, and introduced and established Church
music, rituals and liturgies. The Eastern Orthodox Church
has steadfastly continued on the original path paved by the
Apostles and has preserved the Christian truths and
priceless treasures of the Christian faith throughout Her

> *The Eastern Orthodox Church has until this day
> faithfully observed all these [traditional] things. Can
> one call it stagnation or hardness, when a Church
> community makes it their task to turn all that ancient
> world with its immeasurable depth and inexhaustible
> wealth into a daily reality?*

Mastroyiannopoulos, pp. 95-96 (citing Tyciak, *Zwischen Morgenland
und Abendland.* Duseldorff: n.p. (1949)).

[18] Frangopoulos, pp. 26-30.

[19] The "apocryphal" books are those that the early Church did not
definitively determine were valid.

3

martyred existence. The Eastern Orthodox Church is "the church of the living God, the pillar and bulwark of the truth."[20]

The Eastern Orthodox Church is governed by a synodical system in which bishops or their representatives come together to discuss on an equal basis the common conscience of the people of God and to solve matters of faith and tradition. The first seven ecumenical councils that occurred during the first eight centuries of Christianity[21] were such synods, as the churches, from both East and West, were represented. The Eastern Church believes that the Holy Spirit is present in such an environment and, therefore, affords great respect to the decisions that resulted from these seven synods. These councils discussed the teachings of the Lord in accordance with the Scriptures. Its decisions, when accepted in the conscience of the people of God (the entire Church— clergy and laity alike), became infallible.

---

[20] I Tim. 3:15b.

[21] The first seven Ecumenical Councils are as follows: First Ecumenical Council of Nicea (325 A.D.); Second Ecumenical Council of Constantinople (381 A.D.); Third Ecumenical Council of Ephesus (431 A.D.); Fourth Ecumenical Council of Chaldedon (451 A.D.); Fifth Ecumenical Council of Constantinople (553 A.D.); Sixth Ecumenical Council of Constantinople (680 A.D.); and Seventh Ecumenical Council of Nicea (787 A.D.).

The main teachings of the Eastern Orthodox Church are largely found in the decisions of the first seven ecumenical councils. The first two councils, held in Nicea (325 A.D.) and Constantinople (381 A.D.), were especially significant. Among other important events, the participants drafted and added to the Nicene Creed, the statement of fundamental beliefs affirmed by the faithful at every Baptism and during each Divine Liturgy.

A summary of some of the more important teachings of the Eastern Orthodox Church follows.

1.   Belief in the Holy Trinity. The belief that there is only one God in essence (ουσία) and energy, existing in three distinct, yet equally divine, "hypostases," or Persons,[22] that co-exist, collaborate and co-decide (i.e., "The Father, Son and the Holy Spirit").[23] In the words of St. Gregory the Theologian, the dogma of the Holy Trinity is the "fountainhead of our Faith."

---

[22] Matt. 3:16-17.

[23] Matt. 28:19 (wherein Jesus directed the eleven remaining Apostles to "make disciples of all nations" and to baptize them in the name of the Holy Trinity).

A. God the Father, who is not begotten;[24]

B. God the Son, who was begotten of the Father before the ages;[25] and

C. God the Holy Spirit, who proceeds from the Father,[26] and which, like the Son, is of the very essence of the Father.[27]

2.   The belief that the world (both visible and invisible) was created by God, the Holy Trinity, from nothing (*ex nihilo*) [28] and that all three Persons, the Father through the Son and in the Holy Spirit, took part in the Creation.

---

[24] Rev. 1:8; I Cor. 8:6; John 14:28.

[25] John 1:2; 10:30; 16:28.

[26] John 15:26; Acts 2:33.

[27] I Cor. 2:10; Second Ecumenical Council of Constantinople, canon 5. Unless otherwise indicated, citations to regional councils and to the Ecumenical Councils are from Mastrantonis, *The Sacred Canons*.

[28] "By faith we understand that the world was created by word of God, so that what is seen was made out of things which do not appear." Heb. 11:3.

3.   The belief that man was fashioned by God Himself, in His own image and likeness.[29]

4.   The belief in the distinct but inseparable two natures of Christ: the perfect and complete divine nature and the perfect and complete human nature.[30]

    A. The belief in the distinct divine and human energies and wills of Christ;[31] and

    B. The belief that Jesus Christ was an historic person,[32] sent by the Father out of love to save man;[33] that He died on the Cross and rose from the dead; that He ascended to heaven;[34] and that He

---

[29] Gen. 1:26-27. This personal intervention of God to fashion man, and breathe into him a breath of life, a soul, stands in stark contrast to how He created other things: "Let there be . . ."

[30] John 1:14; Gal. 4:4; Mastrantonis, *The Sacred Canons*, p. 10 (discussing the decisions of the Third Ecumenical Council of Ephesus, as reaffirmed by the Fourth Ecumenical Council of Chalcedon).

[31] Sixth Ecumenical Council of Constantinople.

[32] Luke 3:1 (noting certain leaders who lived during Jesus' time).

[33] John 3:16; Phil. 2:6-7.

[34] I Tim. 3:16.

will come again, in glory, to judge the living and the dead.[35]

5.   The belief that the Holy Scriptures (i.e., the Old and New Testaments) and Ecclesiastical Tradition are of equal importance for salvation and complement one another.[36]

6.   The belief that the Church on earth was founded by Christ[37] as an extension of the Church in heaven for the salvation of man,[38] and was established by the Holy Spirit through the Apostles on the day of Pentecost.[39] The belief that no one can be saved by leading a life inconsistent with the Church.[40]

7.   The belief that the authority of the Church lies within the synodical system, where all bishops are equal,[41]

---

[35] Matt. 25:31-46; II Tim. 4:1.

[36] II Thes. 2:15.

[37] Eph. 1:22-23.

[38] Rev. 21:2; Eph. 5:23.

[39] Acts 2:1-4.

[40] Acts 4:12. In the words of St. Cyprian, "[o]utside the Church, there is no salvation." Danielou, p. 83.

[41] Eph. 2:20; Matt. 20:26-28; Luke 10:19.

and that the Church council decisions are infallible once they are received by the whole Church, clergy and laity.[42]

8.   The belief that salvation comes from faith, works of love,[43] and Divine Grace[44] through the observance of the sacraments (μυστήρια) of the Church. The sacraments are "the sacred ceremonies instituted by God and manifested in visible signs and acts which transmit His invisible Grace."[45] There are seven official sacraments instituted by Christ, or His Apostles, during which the Church invokes the Holy Spirit for sanctification:

  A. Baptism by triple-immersion[46] in water in the name of the Holy Trinity[47] for the remission of sins.[48] Through Baptism we are freed from the

---

[42] Acts 15:6-9.

[43] James 2:17; Gal. 5:6; Eph. 2:10.

[44] Eph. 2:4-5. "Divine Grace" is the benevolence and love that God offers to man.

[45] Mastrantonis, *A New Style of Catechism*, p. 112.

[46] Mastrantonis, *The Sacred Canons*, p. 50 (citing St. Basil the Great, *Epistle to Bishop Amphilochius*, canon 91).

[47] Matt. 28:19.

[48] Rom. 6:3-4.

Original Sin—the sin with which we are all born by virtue of Adam and Eve's fall from the Garden of Eden—and all personal sins. No one can be saved unless he or she is baptized.[49] Unless there is doubt to its canonical administration, baptism in the Holy Trinity is never repeated, for there is "one Lord, one faith, one baptism;"[50]

B. Chrismation by anointing the newly baptized with pre-sanctified Holy Myrrh (described more fully below),[51] which replaced the Apostolic Tradition of "laying on of hands," whereby the sacrament was effected by the physical touch of the clergy;[52]

C. Holy Eucharist, an experience of communion with the Living God, where the plain gifts of the faithful (i.e., leavened bread[53] and pure grape wine) change (μεταβάλλονται) into the very Body and Blood of Jesus Christ with the invocation of the

---

[49] John 3:5; Mark 16:16.

[50] Eph. 4:5.

[51] Eph. 1:13.

[52] Acts 19:5-6; I John 2:20; Acts 8:17. The gifts of Holy Chrismation are many. I Cor. 12:4; Gal. 5:22-23.

[53] Matt. 26:26.

Holy Spirit.[54] After the necessary preparation (i.e., fast and confession),[55] Holy Communion is administered to the faithful, who then come into union with Christ and with one another;

D. Repentance, or Confession,[56] through a face-to-face meeting with the confessor-priest;[57]

E. Ordination of clergy by the laying on of the bishop's hands in an unbroken link of "Apostolic Succession"[58] (i.e., a direct line of ordination from the time of the Apostles). There are three orders of priesthood: deacons, presbyters (priests) and bishops.[59] Deacons and presbyters are allowed to marry before ordination,[60] whereas bishops are obligated to be celibate. By the laying on of hands, canonically ordained clergy receive from Christ,

---

[54] John 6:53-54.

[55] I Cor. 11:27-28.

[56] Luke 15:10; Luke 15:21.

[57] John 20:23; Matt. 18:18; I John 1:9.

[58] Acts 14:23.

[59] Tit. 1:5-9; I Tim. 3:1-10; Phil. 1:1.

[60] Sixth Ecumenical Council of Constantinople, canon 6.

11

"the High Priest," and His Apostles the following three offices: (i) king, to overthrow evil and govern the church; (ii) prophet, to preach the Word; and (iii) priest, to officiate the sacraments and services and reconcile man to God;[61]

F. Marriage, whereby man and woman are united, as the Church is united with Christ in love and honor.[62] The two are bound to one another in the ceremony with symbolic crowns tied together by a ribbon; and

G. Holy Unction, the sacrament of healing during which blessed oil is anointed on the ill by a priest or bishop for the healing of the soul and body.[63]

9.   The belief that the Virgin Mary is the most blessed person[64] among the Apostles, the prophets and all the saints. She was not immaculately conceived;[65] rather, she

---

[61] John 20:21-23; I Tim. 4:14-16.

[62] Eph. 5:21-33.

[63] James 5:14-15; Mark 6:13.

[64] Luke 1:28.

[65] Rom. 3:23; 5:12.

was cleansed from all sin, including the Original Sin,[66] during the Annunciation—where Archangel Gabriel announced to her Christ's impending birth.[67] According to tradition, Virgin Mary died and was buried, but then ascended bodily to heaven since the Lord did not want her sacred body to see decay.

10.	The belief in the resurrection of Christ[68] and the resurrection of the dead.[69] The belief that, after death, the human body returns to the earth, from which it came, while the soul remains in an intermediate stage where it pre-tastes heaven or hell, according to an individual's actions during life. This stage continues until the Second Coming of Christ (also known as the "Last Judgment"), when the resurrection of the dead and the judgment of all who have lived will take place.[70]

---

[66] Luke 1:35.

[67] During the Third Ecumenical Council of Ephesus in 431, the position of Nestorios that Virgin Mary should be called "Christotokos" (Χριστοτόκος), or Mother of Christ, was rejected and it was resolved that Virgin Mary be called "Theotokos" (Θεοτόκος), or Mother of God.

[68] Luke 24:5-7.

[69] I Cor. 15:12; I Thes. 4:16.

[70] I Thes. 4:16-17; Matt. 25:31-46. At first blush, the image of an intermediate stage may conjure images of the West's "purgatory." However, as explained more fully below, belief in this intermediate stage differs sharply from belief in purgatory.

11.   The belief that the just, such as Virgin Mary, the Apostles, the prophets, the martyrs and the saints, have gained their salvation and already have been received into the "Church Triumphant in Heaven."[71]

12.   The belief that there is constant communication between the Church Militant on Earth (which is visible) and the Church Triumphant in Heaven (which is invisible). Integral to the communication of the two Churches are the icons and holy relics of the saints. However, while we ask the saints for intercessions in our prayers and venerate their holy relics and icons, worship belongs only to the Holy Trinity. Thus, the icons adorning the church are not idols to be worshipped but, rather, serve as aids to facilitate our communication with the saints. In essence, "the honor which is given to the icon passes over to the prototype."[72]

13.   The belief that man was created with a free will, enabling him to resist evil.[73] Although God knows one's ultimate destination, God does not predestine someone to a

---

[71] Luke 23:43; Heb.12:22-23.

[72] Mastrantonis, *The Sacred Canons*, p. 18 (citing to the preface of the canons of the Seventh Ecumenical Council of Nicea).

[73] Rom. 13:12.

particular path. One's actions, as well as God's Divine Grace, are important for salvation. Adam fell through the exercise of his free will. The proper use of free will through good works, or "faith working through love,"[74] as Paul said, is critical to man's salvation.

14.   The belief that God cares and provides for man and the created world.[75] God's care is called "Divine Providence."[76]

15.   The belief that there is a balance between the individual's personal freedom and the Church; personal freedom of the faithful is respected, yet communal union is an important facet of the liturgical experience, particularly in the Divine Liturgy.

16.   The belief that all faithful, whether clergy or laity, rich or poor, young or old, together constitute the "royal priesthood,"[77] which operates as the conscience of the entire church and takes on the responsibility of the welfare

---

[74] Gal 5:6; James 2:17.

[75] Ps. 104:27-30; Acts 17:28.

[76] St. Basil the Great, M.P.G. 32:1373.

[77] I Pet. 2:9.

of the church, for we "are all one in Christ Jesus."[78]
While functions differ, [79] both clergy and laity can teach
the Word of God.

17.   Finally, the belief that God has created invisible
intellectual beings, the angels, to glorify God[80] and to
serve God and man.[81] There are two spiritual
classifications of angels, the Good Angels and the Fallen
Angels (i.e., the Devil and his demons). A Good Angel is
assigned by God to each person to assist him or her
towards salvation.[82]

There is perhaps no better description of the
Eastern Orthodox faith than this excerpt from the decrees
of the Seventh Ecumenical Council at Nicea, as recited at
the end of the procession of the holy icons on the first
Sunday of Lent, known as the Sunday of Orthodoxy:

---

[78] Gal. 3:28.

[79] Eph. 4:11-12.

[80] Job 38:7; Χαστούπη, σ. 60.

[81] Heb. 1:14.

[82] Ps. 91:11.

16

*As the Prophets beheld, as the Apostles
have taught, as the Church has received, as
the Teachers have dogmatized, as the
Universe has agreed, as Grace has shown
forth, as the truth was proven, as falsehood
was absolved, as wisdom was presented, as
Christ awarded: Thus we declare, thus we
assert, thus we preach Christ, our true God
. . . This is the Faith of the Apostles. This is
the Faith of the Fathers. This is the Faith
of the Orthodox, this is the Faith which has
established the Universe!*

PART TWO: DIFFERENCES WITH THE ROMAN CATHOLIC CHURCH

I.   The Major Dogmatic Differences

The Eastern Orthodox Church places great emphasis on the first eight centuries of Christianity because it was during this time that the entire Church came together in ecumenical councils to openly discuss fundamental issues, ultimately arriving at certain indisputable truths. Although certain dogmatic differences between East and West have their roots in disputes arising before the last Ecumenical Council of Nicea in 787, these differences became stark and were solidified only thereafter. The main dogmatic differences between the Roman Catholic Church and the Eastern Orthodox Church are described below.

A. The "Filioque"[83]

The word "filioque" derives from the Latin words "filio" (meaning "son") and "que" (meaning "and"). When used in the context of the Nicene Creed, the word

---

[83] For a visual aid to the different views of East and West regarding the hierarchical structure of the Holy Trinity, see Exhibit A.

18

reflects the Roman Catholic Church's contention that the Holy Spirit proceeds from the Father *and from the Son*, and not only from the Father.

Origins of the filioque issue must be examined in the context of what is known as the "Arian heresy." At the First Ecumenical Council in 325 A.D., a priest named Arius from Alexandria, Egypt, posited that the Son was not divine by nature, but by grace. That Council, however, ultimately decided that the Son is of the same essence as the Father and is, therefore, divine by nature. Followers of Arius nevertheless persisted. As a response, and based on St. Basil the Great's treatise "On the Holy Spirit," the Ecumenical Council of Constantinople in 381 A.D. affirmed the original Nicene Creed and added the following to it: "and in the Holy Spirit, the Lord, the Giver of life, who proceeds from the Father, who with the Father and the Son is worshiped and glorified." This credal text was acknowledged as binding in both the East and West. It quickly came "to play a normative role in the definition of faith"[84] and to be recited during the Holy Eucharist.

Certain Western theologians in the third and fourth

---

[84] Filioque Agreed Statement.

centuries discussed the relationship between the Father, Son and Holy Spirit in a way that hinted at the filioque. Nevertheless, it did not appear in any credal text until the local council of Toledo in 589 A.D. This council, convened by Visigoth King Reccard, anathemized those who did not believe that the Holy Spirit proceeds from the Father *and the Son* and mandated that it be recited as such during the Holy Eucharist. It is believed that the King and the bishops present at this council mistakenly believed that the filioque was included in the Greek version of the Creed, as it was affirmed in Constantinople.[85] From Toledo, the recitation of the Creed with the filioque spread throughout much of the western world.

Popes resisted the inclusion of the filioque in the Creed for quite some time. Pope Leo III, in particular, disapproved of its inclusion in the text of the Creed and ordered that the Creed, *without* the filioque, be written on silver shields and hung in Peter's Basilica in Rome.[86] However, the filioque eventually gained general acceptance in the West and, when the Creed was sung at a papal Mass with the filioque in 1014, it received the papal stamp of approval.[87]

---

[85] Ibid.

[86] Παπαδοπούλου, σ. 232; Στεφανίδου, σ. 299.

[87] Filioque Agreed Statement; Στεφανίδου, σ. 374.

There is no direct indication in the Holy Scriptures or elsewhere that the Holy Spirit proceeds from the Son. In fact, the Gospel of John states the following: "But when the Counselor [Holy Spirit] comes, whom I shall send to you from the Father, even the Spirit of truth, *who proceeds from the Father*, he will bear witness to me."[88] The Holy Scriptures further state that Jesus was "exalted at the right hand of God, and [that He] received from the Father the promise of the Holy Spirit."[89] Since the Second Vatican Council (1962-65) (commonly known as "Vatican II"), the Roman Catholic Church has eased its position on filioque and its faithful are free to recite the Nicene Creed without it. In fact, Pope John Paul II recited the Creed in its original Greek form—without the filioque—at Holy

---

[88] John 15:26 (emphasis added).

[89] Acts 2:33. Bishop Kallistos Ware explains the inter-relationship of the Father, Son and Holy Spirit in the following way:

> Just as the Son shows us the Father, so it is the Spirit who shows us the Son, making him present to us. Yet the relation is mutual. The Spirit makes the Son present to us, but it is the Son who sends us the Spirit. (We note that there is a distinction between the "eternal procession" of the Spirit and his "temporal mission". The Spirit is sent into the world, within time, by the Son; *but, as regards his origin within the eternal life of the Trinity, the Spirit proceeds from the Father alone.*)

p. 33 (emphasis added).

Eucharists celebrated in Rome with each of Ecumenical Patriarch Demetrios I in 1987 and Ecumenical Patriarch Bartholomew I in 1995. It is also significant to note that the North American Orthodox-Catholic Theological Consultation met for four years on this topic and, in 2003, published an "agreed statement" which has contributed greatly to a better mutual understanding of the development of the filioque.

B. Papal Supremacy

Another significant difference between the Eastern Orthodox Church and Roman Catholic Church is the latter's contention of the supremacy (πρωτεῖον) of the Pope. As this claim was advanced by the papacy, it became a focal point of division. As noted above, the topic of papal supremacy became particularly intense in the mid-ninth century with the objection by Pope Nicholas I to the election of Photios as Patriarch of Constantinople. According to his contemporary critics, "Nicholas was claiming to be emperor of the whole world."[90]

Subsequent Popes, with the power of the papal bull[91] and local synods, successfully asserted supremacy

---

[90] Στεφανίδου, σ. 345.

[91] The papal "bull" is a papal encyclical sealed with the papal ring.

within the Western Roman Empire, gaining the titles of "Pontifex Maximus" (or, the highest religious authority, an office once held by the Roman Emperor)[92] and, after the Roman Catholic Synod of Trent (Tridento) (1545-63), "Vicar of Christ on Earth."[93] These pronouncements led to the eventual empowerment of the Pope to speak infallibly *ex cathedra*, or "from the throne," as Christ's vicar on Earth.

The West relies on Matthew 16:18 as a biblical basis for the supremacy of the Pope. This verse states the following: "And I tell you, you are Peter, and on this rock (πέτρα)[94] I will build my church." The Roman Catholic Church interprets this passage to mean that Christ viewed Peter as His successor and as the founder upon which He would build His Church. As the Pope is believed by the West to occupy Peter's seat by being the bishop of Rome, it transfers the honor of being Christ's successor from Peter to the Pope.

---

[92] Στεφανίδου, σ. 143.

[93] Παπαγιαννίδου, σ. 123.

[94] "Petros" (Peter) in Greek means "rock."

The East believes that this interpretation is inaccurate and that the Roman Catholic Church has taken Matthew 16:18 out of context. Indeed, the verses preceding Matthew 16:18 place Christ's exclamation in the proper context. The Lord asked all the disciples: "But who do you say that I am? Simon Peter replied, 'You are the Christ, the Son of the living God.' And Jesus answered him . . . And I tell you, you are Peter and on this rock I will build my church."[95] The Eastern Orthodox Church interprets these verses in their entirety to indicate that Jesus was not placing His reliance on Peter to be the foundation of His Church but, rather, was expressing faith in all of his disciples by proclaiming that He would build His Church on the rock-like foundation of His disciples' faith—as illustrated by Peter's reply—that He was the Son of God.

The Roman Catholic Church also employs John 21:15-19 to bolster its claim that the Pope is the successor of Christ. This passage states: "'Simon [Peter], son of John, do you love me more than these?' He said to him, 'Yes, Lord; you know that I love you.' He said to him, 'Feed my lambs.'" The West's reliance on this passage as evidence of Peter's primacy over the other Apostles is

---

[95] Matt. 16:13-18.

misplaced. Rather than suggest Peter's primacy, the passage is indicative of the Apostles' love of Christ and their devotion to Christ until death.[96]

Scholars disagree about Peter's connection to Rome in the first place. In fact, while there is evidence to suggest that Peter preached and was martyred in Rome (likely by Emperor Nero) in about 66 A.D., it is unlikely Peter ever actually served as "bishop" of Rome or acted in any administrative capacity while in Rome.[97] Certain early Fathers refer to Peter as being the first bishop of Rome. Eusebius of Ceasarea, for one, in the third century states that Linus was the first after Peter to be appointed bishop of Rome. However, others, such as St. Irenaeus of Lyon, an early Father who lived at the end of the second century, lists Linus as the first bishop of Rome, after the Apostles (i.e., Peter and Paul) organized Christ's followers and founded the Church. Holy Scripture itself does not directly support the conclusion that Peter was ever bishop of Rome. Among other things, in his Epistle to the Romans, Paul lists the names of twenty-seven persons in Rome to whom he sends greetings;[98] Peter is not among

---

[96] Κολιτσάρα, Η Καινή Διαθήκη, σ. 407 (referring to John 21:18).

[97] Stephanou, p. 13.

[98] Romans ch. 16.

those mentioned. Perhaps this omission is explained by Peter's absence from Rome at that time. Perhaps Peter was never in Rome for any significant period of time. Nevertheless, Scripture remains silent on the point. The importance of Peter's time in Rome and "Petrine Supremacy," as it came to be known, is not Scripturally-based. Rather, it was largely advanced by Pope Leo I in the fifth century.

Peter was indeed a prominent Apostle. He took on a leadership role (as evident in the book of the Acts of the Apostles) and leads the first Jerusalem Church. However, if Peter truly was the sole successor of Christ, why would he refer to himself as "a servant"[99] of God and to Paul as his "beloved brother?"[100] And if the bishop of Rome truly is the successor of Peter, then shouldn't he exhibit the same humility as Peter, who never called himself "Vicar" or proclaimed any supremacy over his brother Apostles? In further contrast to the bishop of Rome, Peter instructs the elders not to be "domineering over those in your charge."[101] Peter was as fallible and human as his

---

[99] II Peter 1:1.

[100] II Peter 3:15.

[101] I Peter 5:1-5.

brethren, who at times criticized him or proved him wrong.[102] Finally, if Peter truly was the infallible leader of the Apostles, then there was no need for the Apostolic Council of Jerusalem in about 50 A.D., where the Apostles and elders of the Church gathered and at which Peter did not appear to preside.[103] In the words of Neilos Kavasilas, a Father of the Eastern Church, "Peter indeed is both Apostle and leader of the Apostles [whereas] . . . the pope is [merely] Bishop of Rome and that is what he is called."[104] Peter may have held a special place for Christ among the Apostles, yet all the Apostles received the authority to teach, to baptize and to forgive sins, as "they were all filled with the Holy Spirit."[105]

The Second Ecumenical Council initially declared the position of bishop of Rome to be "first among equals." However, the Fourth Ecumenical Council declared the position of bishop of New Rome (i.e., Constantinople) to

---

[102] Gal. 2:11-14 (referring to a controversy over Gentile Christians, Paul states in this Epistle: "But when [Peter] came to Antioch I opposed him to his face, because he stood condemned."); Matt.16:23; Stephanou 10-12;.

[103] Acts ch.15; Gal. ch.2.

[104] M.P.G., 149:704-05.

[105] Acts 2:4.

be equal in stature to the Bishop of Rome.[106]
Nevertheless, even these declarations were intended as
rights of honor (πρεσβεία τιμής) to the bishops of the
capital cities of the Roman Empire, and not of authority
and power over the others. At no time have the ancient
Eastern Patriarchates of Constantinople, Alexandria,
Antioch, and Jerusalem, or the new Patriarchates of
Russia, Serbia, Romania and Bulgaria, advanced any
contention of their own supremacy. Moreover, "[a]lthough
the Patriarch of Constantinople has a primacy of honor,
there is no centralized authority corresponding to the
Roman Pope."[107] The Churches that comprise the Eastern
Orthodox Church are independent of one another
administratively, yet united in faith, tradition, sacramental
life, worship, and canonical discipline. As one theologian
has noted, "every bishop possesse[s] the 'seat of
Peter.'"[108]

---

[106] Second Ecumenical Council of Constantinople, canon 3; Fourth
Ecumenical Council of Chalcedon, canon 28; Sixth Ecumenical Council
of Constantinople, canon 36. In relevant part, cannon 28 of the Fourth
Ecumenical Council stated: "The bishop of New Rome shall enjoy the
same honour as the bishop of Old Rome, on account of the removal [i.e.,
move of the east] of the Empire . . . ." Mastrantonis, *The Sacred
Canons*, p. 12.

[107] Mould, p.12.

[108] Meyendorff, *Rome, Constantinople, Moscow*, p. 16.

C. Papal Infallibility

One of the thorniest issues between the Churches is the claim of papal infallibility. The Roman Catholic Church claims that when the Pope acts *ex cathedra* (i.e., from the throne) and proclaims "by a definitive act a doctrine pertaining to faith or morals"[109] his words and actions are infallible, as if the Pope were Christ Himself speaking and acting.

Although not on the intended agenda, this claim became dogma in the Roman Catholic Church at the First Vatican Council of Rome in 1870. That Council declared the following:

> *Jesus Christ has three existences. His personal existence, which Arius denied; His mystical existence in the Sacrament of the Holy Eucharist, which Calvin denied; and His other existence, which completes the first two and through which He lives constantly, namely His authority in the person of His Vicar on Earth. The Council, maintaining this third existence, assures the world that it possesses Jesus Christ.*

---

[109] *Catechism of the Catholic Church*, paragraph 891.

As historians note, this declaration coincides with the ethnic uprising and political independence of the peoples of Western Europe, especially in Italy.[110] One historical view is that the bishop of Rome acted to extend his claim of supremacy to one of infallibility at a time when his earthly authority was threatened by elevating his seat above any political office or synod.

in any event, the claim of papal infallibility does not rest well with history. In particular, it is difficult to reconcile the notion that men occupying a position from which their predecessors have been deposed may speak infallibly, even *ex cathedra*.[111] More importantly, papal infallibility destroys the "conscience of the Church," as it flies in the face of the historical acceptance of council decisions as the "supreme authority and the infallible guidance to proclaim the truth of Salvation."[112] As discussed above, the East believes that only bodies such as the ecumenical councils, those collegial bodies of

---

[110] *See* Παπαδοπούλου, σ. 298-299.

[111] Κολιτσάρα, Η Δυτική Εκκλησία, σ. 67; Στεφανίδου, σ. 486-487.

[112] Mastrantonis, *What is the Eastern Orthodox Church?*, p. 31. Eastern theologians believe that the concept of infallibility also negatively affects the office of the bishop (*see, e.g.*, Παπαδοπούλου, p. 317), as any bishop under an infallible Pope may be viewed as a representative of the Pope and not of Christ.

discourse that existed during the first eight centuries of Christianity, can, with the presence of the Holy Spirit, arrive at decisions which, once accepted by both the clergy and laity, become accepted truths of the infallible Church.

D. The Synodical System

Based on the experience of the Apostolic church,[113] Eastern Orthodox bishops continued to expect collegiality in their regional councils and synods. In contrast, Roman Catholic bishops historically have not had equal rights in councils. Indeed, the Pope alone can call a council and set its agenda, while the body of bishops has only as much authority as the Pope permits.[114] As a result, the councils that occurred after 1054 often focused on strengthening the papacy. A notable exception to this was Vatican II, which was conducted in a spirit of brotherhood, "self-criticism" and "re-examination."[115] Nevertheless, even at Vatican II, concern regarding the problem of papal authority and the lack of collegiality

---

[113] *See* Acts ch. 15.

[114] Meyendorff, *Orthodoxy and Catholicity*, p. 162.

[115] Putz, pp. 322-23.

among the bishops were not addressed.[116] Moreover, the Roman Curia, the elite court charged with advising the Pope on important matters, "remained a block"[117] to attempts to decentralize power. Hence, despite the progress of Vatican II, the Roman Catholic Church continues to view itself much like a "monarchy with the Bishop of Rome as its supreme controlling authority."[118]

II.   The Major Liturgical Differences

A. Holy Eucharist

1. The Epiclesis

At the Last Supper, the Lord instituted the change of simple bread and wine into His very Body and Blood with the words of Institution: "Take, eat; this is my body. . . . Drink of it, all of you; for this is my blood of the covenant, which is poured out for many for the forgiveness of sins."[119]

---

[116] A Roman Catholic scholar, Hans Küng (at the time Director of the Institute for Ecumenical Research) claimed that the offices of the bishops and of the Pope at Vatican I were parallel to those of the bishops and the Pope at Vatican II in that, in both cases, the supremacy of the Pope was by the will of God ("Θείω δικαίω"). Καλογήρου, σ. 73.

[117] Putz, p. 325.

[118] Harakas, p.165.

[119] Matt. 26:26-28.

32

The Eastern Orthodox Divine Liturgy contains a prayer of invocation, or epiclesis, which immediately follows the words of Institution and through which the priest asks God the Father to send the Holy Spirit to change[120] (να μεταβάλη) the plain gifts of the people into the Holy Gifts of the very Body and Blood of Jesus Christ.[121]

Although the epiclesis is as ancient as the liturgies of the Apostolic Fathers,[122] the Roman Catholic Church dispensed with the invocation of the Holy Spirit, maintaining only the words of Institution for the point of

---

[120] This conversion is commonly referred to in the Roman Catholic Church as "transubstantiation." Faced with challenges concerning the Holy Eucharist by Protestant reformers, the Council of Trent proclaimed in chapter 4 of Session 13: "Because Christ our Redeemer declared that what He offered under the species of bread was truly His Body, it has always been the faith of the Church of God (and this holy Synod now states it again) that by the consecration of the bread and wine a change takes place in which the entire substance of the bread is changed into the substance of the Body of Christ our Lord, and the entire substance of the wine into the substance of His Blood. This change the Holy Catholic Church fittingly and properly calls 'transubstantiation.'"

[121] In St. John Chrysostom's Divine Liturgy, the epiclesis reads as follows: "Again we offer to Thee this rational and bloodless Worship, and we beseech Thee, and pray, and supplicate Thee: send down Thy Holy Spirit upon us, and upon these Gifts here presented. And make this Bread the Precious Body of Thy Christ. And that which is in this Cup, the Precious Blood of Thy Christ. Changing (them) by Thy Holy Spirit. Amen, Amen, Amen." Papadeas, p. 30.

[122] Καλλινίκου, σ. 347; Ireneus, M.P.G. 91:7,1253.

33

consecration.[123] The Eastern Orthodox Church views this as incomplete. In the words of one theologian, "the authentic 'Eastern' formulation of doctrine is that the invocation [epiclesis] consecrates the eucharist. By the action of the Holy Spirit upon the elements the communicants receive the Body and Blood of Christ."[124] In fact, the Eastern Orthodox Church believes that the laity itself is intimately involved in the consecration through their responses of "Amen"[125] to the invocations. The faithful "are ordained into the ministry of Christ to the world . . . through participation in the offering of Christ's sacrifice on behalf of the world . . . [T]he entire assembly, in the mutual submission of all ministries one to another, constitutes a single body for the realization of the

---

[123] *The Sacramentary*, p. 545.

[124] Dix, p. 296.

[125] The importance of the laity's involvement through the "Amen" has been emphasized throughout Christian times. For instance, St. Justin the Martyr in the mid-second century stated in his First Apology (ch. 65). "And when he has concluded the prayers and thanksgivings, all the people present express their assent by saying amen." As Metropolitan John of Pergamon notes, "it is forbidden to celebrate the Eucharist without a gathering of the people, without the people's 'Amen'." Zizioulias, pp. 36-37.

[126] Schmemann, *The Eucharist*, p. 93 (italics omitted). As St. Clement, third bishop of Rome, stated at the end of the first century, "We too, then, should gather together for worship . . . as it were with one mouth, that we may share in his great and glorious promises." Richardson, p. 59 (citing Clement's First Letter).

34

priesthood of Jesus Christ."[126] In effect, the Eastern Orthodox priest, representing the whole community and with the direct involvement of the laity, presents himself as an instrument of the Holy Spirit to effectuate the conversion. As Dr. Gregory Dix states: "Looking at the matter purely historically, I cannot help thinking that the Greeks [the Eastern Orthodox Church] are, from their own point of view, entirely right, and ought to be allowed to know their own tradition better than their Western imitators."[127]

2. Leavened and Unleavened Bread

The Roman Catholic Church after the eighth century adopted the theory that the Last Supper was a Passover Seder and, therefore, began to use unleavened bread in the Holy Eucharist. This practice runs contrary to the teachings of the New Testament and the actions of Christ and the Apostles. The teaching of the ancient Church was that the Last Supper itself took place before Passover (specifically, on Thursday evening before Passover), since, on the day of preparation for Passover Jesus was already dead and buried.[128] Jesus Christ,

---

[127] Dix, p. 296 (discussing the Eastern teaching on the Invocation).

[128] *See* Matt. 27:62; Mark 15:42-43; Luke 23:54; John 19:31-42. For more information on this issue see Mathews, p. 8.

therefore, could not have partaken in the Passover Meal that year. Indeed, the Last Supper was a distinct supper at which Jesus instituted Holy Communion. Additional evidence that the Last Supper was not a Seder comes from the meal itself. In particular, the Gospels note that Jesus used "bread" (ἄρτον) and do not refer to "matzo" (ἄζυμα), which is the ritualistic unleavened bread used in the Jewish Passover meal. As Luke describes in his Gospel, "[H]e took bread, and when he had given thanks he broke it and gave it to them."[129]

3. The Lord's Blood

Around the tenth century, the Roman Catholic Church prohibited laypeople from receiving the precious Blood of the Lord in the Holy Eucharist celebration.[130] In the sixteenth century Synod of Trent, the Roman Catholic Church officially forbade laypersons from receiving Holy Communion directly from the Cup containing the Blood of

---

[129] Luke 22:19.

[130] Stephanou, p. 21.

[131] Κολιτσάρα, Η Δυτική Εκκλησία, σ. 93 (citing Ὑακίνθου Γάγ, Μεγάλη Κατήχησις, Μέρος Γ', σ. 73). It is interesting to note that the Synod of Trent not only denied that there is a divine command that all faithful should receive Holy Eucharist under both forms (i.e., wine as well as bread) and that Holy Eucharist is a necessary sacrament for young children, but also condemned those who denied "concomitantia" (discussed below).

Christ.[131] Rather, the faithful were permitted to receive only the Body in the form of a small wafer, while the Cup was reserved for the clergy. It is believed that the reason for this restriction was to provide distinction to the priesthood and distinguish the clergy from the laity.[132] The Roman Catholic Church contends that the laity nevertheless continues to receive both species of the Holy Gifts by receiving the wafer under the theory of "concomitantia," in which the Blood is believed to be contained within the Body.[133] The Second Vatican Council, however, revisited the decisions of the Synod of Trent and allowed for the lay faithful to receive the Blood from the Cup, if they so choose.

The Eastern Orthodox Church believes that withholding the Cup from laypeople is unjustified. The Lord Himself not only referred specifically to the drinking of His Blood when He established Holy Communion,[134] but also noted its importance to those gathered to hear him

---

[132] Κολιτσάπα, Η Δυτική Εκκλησία, σ. 93. Another reason for the change in administering Holy Eucharist was to prevent spilling by laypeople partaking from the chalice. Indeed, the Eastern Church also struggled with this issue and arrived at the use of the spoon to administer the Blood and Body together as a solution. Καλλινίκου, σ. 188-89.

[133] Θεοδώρου, p. 10.

[134] Matt. 26:27 ("Drink of it, all of you . . .").

teach at in the synagogue at Capernaum, stating, "Truly, truly, I say to you, unless you eat the flesh of the Son of man and drink his blood, you have no life in you."[135]

4. Multiple Celebrations of Holy Eucharist

After the eighth century, the Roman Catholic Church broke from centuries of practice by allowing the same priest to celebrate more than one liturgy on the same day on the same Holy Table.[136] St. Ignatius of Antioch in Chapter 4 of his 107 A.D. letter to the Philadelphians states, "One Holy Eucharist is needed." Church historian Sergios Makraios further explains: "one is the sacrificed and one the sacrificer . . . one is the day of sacrifice . . .

---

[135] John 6:53.

[136] Although certain differences relating to the Holy Table, exist between East and West, both Churches continue to place the bread and wine for Holy Communion on the Holy Table. The Holy Table, also called the "altar" or "Thysiasterion" (i.e., place of sacrifice), is a table in the Sanctuary where the Greatest Sacrifice, the sacrifice of our Lord, takes place. Early Church historian Eusebius refers to it as that "Holy place of sacrifice of the saints placed in the middle [of the church]." M.P.G. 20,865. In fact, the ancient church developed the practice of celebrating the Holy Eucharist on the tombs of martyrs. St. Augustine speaks about the tomb of St. Cyprian being used as such. See M.P.L. 38,1413. This practice inspired the tradition of all Holy Tables being consecrated with the relics of at least one martyr or saint of the Church. See Seventh Ecumenical Council of Nicea, canon 7; Καλλινίκου, σ. 121.

here is one place of sacrifice, Golgotha [i.e., the Holy Table] . . . one is the cup."[137]

5. *Private Mass*

In the Eastern Orthodox Church, the celebrant during the epiclesis represents all the faithful, using the word "we" in asking God the Father to send the Holy Spirit so that it may change the bread and wine. In contrast, the Roman Catholic priest is permitted to perform the mass by himself and call the service "his" mass. From the Eastern Orthodox point of view, it is impossible for one person, even a canonically ordained priest, to conduct the Divine Liturgy alone, or for himself, because the Holy Eucharist is celebrated by the whole Church, it is a gathering of believers for a feast, a synaxis.

C. Facing the East

In the Eastern Church, the officiating clergy and the faithful during the Divine Liturgy both face the Holy Table, which, where feasible, faces the east. St. Basil the

---

[137] Καλλινίκου, σ. 124-25.

[138] Mastrantonis, *The Sacred Canons*, p. 50 (citing St. Basil the Great, *Epistle to Bishop Amphilochius*, canon 91). Others say that the clergy and faithful look towards the East, from where the natural light (i.e., the Sun) rises.

Great says that we pray "toward the East, to denote, that we are in quest of Eden, that garden in the East from whence our first parents were rejected."[138] Also, the Holy Vessel (also known in the Roman Catholic Church as the "Tabernacle") where the Reserved Sacrament (i.e., Holy Communion) is kept, in part, for emergencies, is placed on the eastern side of the Holy Table and provides the continuous presence of the Lord Himself. In contrast, officiating Roman Catholic clergy face the faithful during the Holy Eucharist and the Holy Vessel is typically located not on the Holy Table, but in the altar wall, or elsewhere.

D. The Sign of the Cross

The followers of the Roman Catholic Church perform the sign of the cross using a virtually open right palm and by moving the hand from the forehead, to the abdomen, and then from the left shoulder to the right shoulder. Orthodox faithful perform the sign of the cross with the tips of the right thumb, index finger and middle finger touching (representing the Father, Son and Holy Spirit), and the remaining two fingers pressed against the palm (representing the two natures of Christ, human and divine), moving the hand up, down, and then right to left. One pious interpretation of these movements is as follows: up to praise the Holy Trinity in heaven; down to worship the Lord Jesus Christ, who came from heaven through the belly of Virgin Mary for us; to the right shoulder to ask the Lord to put us at His right side with the saints and, lastly, to the left, so as not to be placed with the sinners.[139] In this way, we give glory to Christ, who extended His hands on the Cross for us.

E. Icons

From the beginning of Christianity, the faithful employed symbols such as the cross, the lamb, the anchor, the vineyard, and the shepherd to express Christian themes. As Christianity emerged triumphant in the fourth century, representational art forms depicting historical people, most notably in painted icons, became increasingly prevalent in the church.[140]

---

[139] Καντιώτου, σ. 141-42

[140] During the period of turmoil known as the iconoclastic controversy (726-878 A.D.), however, the veneration of icons was considered by some to be idolatry, and many icons were destroyed. It is interesting to note that this controversy continued for several decades after the Seventh Ecumenical Council decreed in 787 A.D. that icons held a rightful place in the church. "The Council decided icons were like the Holy Scriptures and worthy of honor and veneration." Hallick, p 27. Specifically, the Council declared: "The figure of the cross and holy images, whether made in colors of stone, or of any other material are to be retained. They are not to become objects of adoration in the proper sense, which is given to God alone, but they are useful because they raise the mind of the congregation to the objects which they represent."

41

Icons are not idols and, as such, they are not worshipped, only *venerated,* as worship belongs only to the Holy Trinity. The veneration of icons in the Eastern Orthodox Church has deep and complex meaning. The human being is a composite—body and soul, flesh and spirit. Yet, strict Byzantine icons depict human subjects with frail, drawn-out features so that the focus of the viewer is not on the carnal beauty of the face or physical characteristics of the subject but, rather, on the subject's spiritual being. As one scholar notes, "[t]he Byzantine icon is a formal kind of art intent on 'an abstract expression of religious emotion,' divorced from nature, a reaction against the worldliness and secularization of life (non-representational)."[141]

Icons are "windows to heaven," tools through which historical and dogmatic truths are expressed. Icons help the faithful achieve a spiritual understanding that transcends the worldly people and events they depict. For

---

[141] Constantelos, p. 23. The Byzantine era is known as the "Golden Age of Iconography," and it made popular not only the individual icon but also religious paintings on canvas and mosaics on church walls. Byzantine art and architecture "dematerializes" bodies and structures, eliminating ground lines and real space. One example of this is the columns in the cathedral of St. Sophia in Constantinople, which are curved in such a way as to displace the weight and give the impression that the entire church is hanging from the heavens.

instance, "the Pantocrator (i.e., the icon of Christ in the dome) depicts at once the Father and the Son—the expression of dogma concerning consubstantiality."[142] Also, the Platytera (i.e., Virgin Mary) in the apse in back of the Sanctuary, known as the niche, expresses the Incarnation of our Lord (in other words, the union of God and man in Christ) by depicting Virgin Mary holding Jesus Christ as a child in her lap.

Icons play an important role in worship, providing a link of communication between the Church militant on earth and the Church triumphant in heaven. The angels, the saints and the faithful unite in the glorification of God. We are not alone in prayer; rather, we are surrounded by "a great cloud of witnesses eager to see our progression in our faith and ready to steady us when we stumble."[143] Persons depicted in the icons are examples and heroes of faith for the faithful.

While the Eastern Orthodox Church has avoided three-dimensional representations of humans, the Roman Catholic Church began using statues to decorate its churches after the eighth century. Also, the Renaissance

---

[142] Kalokyris, p. 15.

[143] Knapp, p. 5. *See also* Heb. 12:1-2.

produced in the West more natural, picture-like paintings and representations, with life-like round faces and full bodies. As worldly art, these portrayals are certainly more rational and accurate. Yet Byzantine-style iconography more readily permits the viewer to grasp what lies beyond the senses.

III. The Major Sacramental Differences

A. Baptism

1. Baptism by Infusion

Until the late Middle Ages, both East and West performed the sacrament of Baptism by triple-immersion (i.e., immersing the baptized three times in water) in the name of the Holy Trinity to symbolize the three day burial and resurrection of Jesus Christ.[144] The Greek word "baptizo" means nothing less than "I immerse." By being immersed, or buried, under water, the baptized is "buried" as the Lord was and by ascending from the water arises from death, leaving all sins behind under water.[145] In

---

[144] Note that the Eastern Orthodox priest in performing the Baptism (and, in fact, in performing all sacraments) uses the third person: "The servant of God, [the baptized's name], is baptized . . ." In this way, the priest acknowledges that the Lord, and not the priest, is performing the sacrament. In contrast, the Roman Catholic priest uses the first person: "I baptize you . . ."

about the fourteenth century, the Roman Catholic Church began administering Baptism by the sprinkling or pouring (also known as "infusion") of sanctified water over the baptized. The East views the Roman Catholic practice of baptizing by infusion to be unjustified. Indeed, the Lord Himself entered the Jordan River for Baptism; he was not infused with water.[146] The Eastern Church does, however, permit infusion, and even Baptism in the air (i.e., lifting the baptized in the air three times in the name of the Holy Trinity), in cases of grave emergencies. Nevertheless, if one is infused and survives the immediate danger, his or her Baptism must be completed, although the priest must not duplicate what was said or done at the emergency Baptism.

2. Separation of Chrismation and Holy Communion from Baptism

Chrismation, a rite administered along with Baptism and Holy Communion in the early Church, in the Eastern Orthodox Church consists of the anointment of the

---

[145] "Do you not know that all of us who have been baptized into Christ Jesus were baptized into his death? We were buried therefore with him by baptism into death, so that as Christ was raised from the dead by the glory of the Father, we too might walk in newness of life." Rom. 6:3-4.

[146] Matt. 3:16.

baptized with myrrh. Holy Myrrh, which is called "the seal of the gift (σφραγίς δωρεάς) of the Holy Spirit,"[147] is comprised of a mixture of olive oil and approximately forty aromatic oils taken from various flowers and plants; the many ingredients symbolize the many gifts of the Holy Spirit.[148]

In the early Church, Chrismation was administered by the local bishop "by two means (1) the laying on of hands and prayer and (2) by anointing. In the East, the practice of administering this sacrament through anointing prevailed."[149] As the number of chatecumenate Christians increased, bishops were not able to travel to all areas and be present for all the sacraments of initiation. The East responded by permitting priests to perform the sacrament of Chrismation with pre-sanctified Holy Myrrh, thus continuing the practice of administering Baptism and Chrismation together. The Roman Catholic Church did

---

[147] Eph. 1:13-14.

[148] Most of the Eastern Orthodox Churches receive Holy Myrrh consecrated by the Ecumenical Patriarchate in Constantinople (Istanbul). The Holy Myrrh is consecrated in a special ceremony performed every few years during Holy Week by His All Holiness the Ecumenical Patriarch, assisted by members of the Holy Synod and representatives of the autocephalous churches.

[149] Coniaris, *These Are the Sacraments*, p. 56 (citation omitted). Note that the Apostles administered Chrismation by the laying on of the hands. Acts 8:17; 19:6.

not give this right to the priests and, as a result, youths were required to wait until they were older to be Chrismated (or "Confirmed", as it is known in the Roman Catholic Church) by the bishop.[150] Today, while the bishop remains the "ordinary" minister of Confirmation in the Roman Catholic Church, the Sacrament may also be performed by priests; the Confirmation is administered in two parts, the laying on of hands and annointing the forehead with chrism.Note that following the separation of Chrismation from Baptism, the Roman Catholic Church also began giving Holy Communion to a child for the first time at the medieval "age of reason," or at about the age of seven.[151]

The East believes that the sacraments of Chrismation and Holy Communion are inseparable from Baptism and that Holy Tradition demands[152] that Chrismation be administered as soon as the baptized is raised the third time from the water. As the Council of

---

[150] White, pp. 200-01.

[151] "In the case of infant baptism, medieval Latin practice separated this unity action, deferring confirmation by the bishop and Eucharistic communion to a later date." Baptism Agreed Statement. Παπαγιαννίδου, σ. 144.

[152] "As soon as you come up from the water you are given a pure white garment. . . . Then, you come immediately to the bishop to receive the final sealing." Coniaris, *These Are the Sacraments*, p. 53 (quoting Theodore of Mopsuestia from the fourth century).

Laodicea decreed in the fourth century, "Those illuminated should after their baptism be anointed."[153] In fact, the North American Orthodox-Catholic Theological Consultation Agreed Statement on "Baptism and 'Sacramental Economy'" states the following:

> *[I]nitiation into the Church was understood as a single action with different "moments." Thus, in Acts 2:38-42 we find baptism with water directly followed by the reception of the Holy Spirit [i.e., Chrismation] and "the breaking of bread" (Eucharist) by the community . . .*

The Eastern Church has continued the tradition of administering all three sacraments of initiation—Baptism, Chrismation and Holy Communion—in one rite. This is consistent with how the sacraments were administered in the Apostolic Tradition of Hippolytus in about 216 A.D.[154] The Eastern Church believes that young children should

---

[153] Mastrantonis, *The Sacred Canons*, p. 33 (Regional Council of Laodicea, canon 48).

[154] *See* Easton, pp. 45-49. "This continuity between the various stages of initiation is consistently reproduced in the oldest liturgical texts and in early patristic witnesses . . ." Baptism Agreed Statement. Note that certain Eastern Church priests choose to administer Holy Eucharist to the newly baptized during the same ceremony, using Holy Eucharist from the Reserved Sacrament, while others administer Holy Eucharist to the newly baptized on the Sunday following the Baptismal ceremony.

not be deprived of Holy Communion and Chrismation, which, as is evident from the following passages from Gospel of John, are critical sacraments: "unless one is born of water and the Spirit [i.e., Baptism and Chrismation], he cannot enter the kingdom of God"[155] and "unless you eat the flesh of the Son of man and drink his blood [i.e., take Holy Communion], you have no life in you."[156] Every baptized person, unless canonically sanctioned, is a full member of the body of Christ and must not be denied the blessings of Chrismation and Holy Communion.

It is important to note that there have been recent efforts in the Roman Catholic Church to restore the union of the three sacraments of initiation. *The People's Catechism—Catholic Faith for Adults*, a document relating to the modern catechism in the Roman Catholic Church, states the following:

> *After Vatican II, and with the help of serious historical, theological, and pastoral investigation, the reform of the rites of initiation has been undertaken. The catechumenate has been restored. A rite of*

---

[155] John 3:5.

[156] John 6:53.

*infant baptism, designed for babies, is
being developed. The age of Confirmation
is under discussion, with many leaning to a
restoration of its modest relationship to
Baptism. And the ancient order and unity
of the three sacraments of initiation is
informing both theological debate and
pastoral practice.*[157]

B. Confession

The pattern of sin is unfortunately quite natural for
humans. As Paul lamented: "I do not understand my own
actions. For I do not do what I want, but I do the very
thing I hate."[158] Penance and the sacrament of Confession
were developed to enable Christians to atone for and
correct sin. In practice, beginning in the twelfth century,
Confession in the Roman Catholic Church generally began
taking place in a booth with a screen separating the
confessed and the confessor-priest. Vatican II, however,
reestablished that Confession may be administered in the
original manner commonly practiced by the early Church
before the Great Schism, i.e., as a face-to-face meeting
between the confessed and the confessor-priest. The
advantage of this practice, as it continues to exist in the

---

[157] Lucker et al., p. 150.

[158] Rom. 7:15.

East, is that it requires the penitent to be more genuinely contrite by facing the confessor-priest, who acts in accordance with the authority vested in him by the Lord.[159] It also permits the confessor-priest to better evaluate the character of the penitent and better communicate advice and forgiving prayers.

C. Holy Unction

As is evident from St. James' Epistle, Holy Unction was intended as the healing Sacrament: "Is any among you sick? Let him call for the elders of the church, and let them pray over him, anointing him with oil in the name of the Lord; and the prayer of faith will save the sick man."[160] The Roman Catholic Church in the eleventh began using Holy Unction as the "last rite" (i.e., after penance and before death) for the dying century to reduce the possibility of sin by the anointed person after its administration. However, the Second Vatican Council recognized it as a sacrament for anointing the sick and the Roman Catholic Church thus no longer reserves it for

---

[159] "If you forgive the sins of any, they are forgiven; if you retain the sins of any, they are retained." John 20:23. Luke describes the importance of repentance and confession in the following way: "[T]here is joy before the angels of God over one sinner who repents." Luke 15:10.

[160] James 5:14-15; *see also* Mark 6:13.

near-death situations; actually, for the most part, it no longer even calls it a "last rite". The Eastern Church has continued the early Church tradition of using Holy Communion to the dying (although not officially as a "last rite") and Holy Unction (known as euchelaion, or "prayer-oil") as the healing sacrament for the sick.[161]

D. Marriage

1. Marriage Between Eastern Orthodox and Roman Catholic Christians

The Eastern Orthodox Church does not currently recognize as valid the sacrament of marriage performed in the Roman Catholic Church; rather, an Eastern Orthodox Christian who marries outside the Church does not remain in "good standing" with the Church and cannot receive Holy Communion. The Eastern Orthodox Church will, however, perform the sacrament of marriage between Eastern Orthodox and Roman Catholic Christians.

After Vatican II, the Roman Catholic Church began recognizing certain sacraments, including marriage, which had been performed in the Eastern Orthodox Church. As a result, the U.S. Theological Consultation between the two

---

[161] At times, it is not possible to administer Holy Eucharist to a sick person by the mouth. In these cases, Holy Unction is sometimes administered to the sick by the Eastern Orthodox priest.

Churches recommended in 1971 "that the [Roman] Catholic Church, as a normative practice, allow the Catholic party to be married with the Orthodox priest officiating."[162]

2. Celibacy of the Clergy

The First (325 A.D.) and Sixth (680 A.D.) Ecumenical Councils decided to allow marriage for priests, so long as the marriage occurred prior to ordination. [163] Nevertheless, "[s]ince the sixth century bishops have been selected from the celibate clergy."[164] The Eastern Orthodox Church has continued the early Church traditions of allowing its priests to marry and selecting its bishops from the celibate clergy.

At the Second Lateran Council of 1139, the Roman Catholic Church forbade marriage for all clergy. One reason advanced for this decision was to enable clergy to devote themselves solely to the Church, although another

---

[162] Agreed Statement on Marriage.

[163] The Sixth Ecumenical Council stated in its canon 13 that "Although the Romans wish that everyone ordained deacon or Presbyter should put away his wife, we wish the marriages of deacons and presbyters to continue valid and firm." Mastrantonis, *The Sacred Canons*, p. 13. However, that same Council added in its canon 12 that "no one ordained a bishop shall any longer live with his wife." Ibid.

[164] Litsas, pp. 48-49.

reason appears to have been a response to concerns that legitimate children of clergy might inherit Church lands.

3. Divorce

The Roman Catholic Church does not issue divorces, but does issue annulments in certain cases. However, we know that the Lord leaves room for divorce "on the ground of unchastity."[165] The Eastern Orthodox Church with much pain issues divorces in situations involving adultery and abandonment, or other circumstances in which the marriage is determined by a spiritual court to be irreparably broken.

4. Abortion

Both churches generally consider abortion a grave sin. While the Roman Catholic Church has indicated that abortion is a sin even in situations where the life of the mother is in danger, the Eastern Church has not spoken definitively on this issue.

---

[165] Matt. 5:32.

IV.   Differences Relating to Virgin Mary

A. Immaculate Conception

Throughout the centuries, the Roman Catholic Church has given great attention and honor to the person of Virgin Mary. This attention culminated in the teaching of the "Immaculate Conception" of Virgin Mary (i.e., that Virgin Mary was born without the Original Sin), which became dogma by papal degree in 1854, before the First Vatican Council. The Western Church adopted the Augustinian concept of the fall of Adam and Eve from Paradise, hence viewing the Original Sin as "some physical 'taint' of [inherent] guilt."[166] The Roman Catholic Church felt that Virgin Mary could not be part of such guilt, and therefore came up with the teaching of Immaculate Conception.[167] In contrast, the Eastern Orthodox Church views the Original Sin as "'the ancestral curse' by which human beings were alienated from the divine life."[168] In other words, "we are born into an environment where it is easy to do evil and hard to do good."[169]

---

[166] Ware, p. 62.

[167] Ibid., p. 77.

[168] Pulcini, p. 16.

[169] Ware, p. 62.

The concept of the Immaculate Conception is unfounded and contrary to the Scriptures, which state that all humans are born with the Original Sin.[170] In fact, "[e]ven theologians of the Western Church . . . opposed this teaching."[171] The teaching of the early Church, continued by the Eastern Orthodox Church, is that Virgin Mary is the most blessed person among the prophets, saints and Apostles.[172] Nevertheless, like all humans, she was born with the Original Sin but was cleansed of all sin during the Annunciation, thus making the conception and birth of *Christ* "immaculate."[173] In short, the Eastern Orthodox Church considers Virgin Mary the link between the Old and New Testaments, "the last and greatest of the righteous men and women of the Old Covenant . . . She is for us the supreme offering made by the human race to God."[174]

---

[170] Rom. 5:12-14.

[171] Kokkinakis, p. 13. Among the contemporary figures opposing the teaching of Immaculate Conception was Thomas Aquinas.

[172] Indeed, Archangel Gabriel referred to Virgin Mary as the "favored one". Luke 1:28. Also, during the Divine Liturgy we sing: "Especially for our most holy, pure, most blessed, glorious Lady, Theotokos, and Ever-Virgin Mary." Papadeas, p. 31.

[173] In the words of St. Luke, "And the angel said to her, 'The Holy Spirit will come upon you, and the power of the Most High will overshadow you; therefore the child to be born will be called holy, the Son of God.'" Luke 1:35.

B. The Dormition

The Roman Catholic Church also teaches that the body of Virgin Mary was never buried but, rather, was assumed to heaven following her death. This teaching became dogma relatively recently, in 1950, during the papacy of Pius XII. [175]

According to tradition, Virgin Mary died and was buried in the town of Gethsemane with all the Apostles present. The Eastern Orthodox Church believes that the Lord did not want her body to decay and, therefore, raised it to heaven. This belief has not been consecrated as dogma but is supported by centuries of iconography and hymnology.

---

[174] Ware, pp. 77-78. It is relevant to note that Vatican II discussed the issue of how to regard Virgin Mary, but decided only "to place her as a member of the Church under the headship of Jesus Christ." Putz, p. 324.

[175] Coniaris, *Introducing the Orthodox Church*, p. 101; Keifer, p. 5. The document establishing this Roman Catholic doctrine, the *Munificentissimus Deus*, was promulgated by Pius XII on November 1, 1950, and states: "The Immaculate Mother of God, the ever-Virgin Mary, having completed the course of her earthly life, was assumed body and soul into heavenly glory."

V. Differences Relating to Death and the Afterlife

Differences also arose between East and West with respect to beliefs and traditions relating to the dead and the afterlife.

A. Cremation

Both churches offer prayers for the dead, a practice found in the early Christian liturgies.[176] These prayers express love and remembrance for the dead and ask the Lord to be merciful to them at the Last Judgment. However, since 1963, the Roman Catholic Church has permitted cremation. The Eastern Orthodox Church, adhering more strictly to Scripture (for instance, "you are

---

[176] In the Greek Orthodox Church, prayers for the dead are elaborate and include special memorial services at the end of the Divine Liturgy, called "Mnemosyna" (Μνημόσυνα). Mnemosyna are typically performed at certain intervals following the death (usually on the fortieth day after death and on the six-month, one-year and three-year anniversaries). A tray with boiled wheat, decorated with sugar-coated almonds, called "kollyva" (κόλλυβα), is brought to the Church by the survivors and/or friends of the deceased. Kollyva symbolize the inevitable resurrection of the deceased, as "unless a grain of wheat falls into the earth and dies, it remains alone; but if it dies, it bears much fruit." John 12:24; I Cor. 15:35-37. The first name of the deceased is mentioned by the priest during the Mnemosyno, and the kollyva are blessed and then distributed to the faithful, who, upon their receipt, say, "May the Lord forgive his/her sins."

dust, and to dust you shall return"[177]), generally views cremation as a rejection of the resurrection. As Christ was buried, so should we be.

B. Purgatory

The early Church taught that between death and the Last Judgment the soul entered an "intermediate stage" in which it "pre-tasted" heaven and hell based on the person's actions during life. The Roman Catholic Church since the thirteenth century has taught that certain souls must spend time after death in "purgatory," an intermediate place or phase where, among other things, such souls go through "fire" to atone for their sins and enter Paradise. This teaching is based largely on the mention of "fire" in I Corinthians, where Paul stated: "If any man's work is burned up, he will suffer loss, though he himself will be saved, but only as through fire."[178] A past Roman Catholic practice associated with purgatory is the sale of indulgences, whereby the Roman Catholic Church claimed it had the ability to draw upon—for a price—the endless treasury of spiritual merits (thesaurus meritorium) of Christ, Virgin Mary and the saints to

---

[177] Gen. 3:19.

[178] I Cor. 3:15.

forgive sins on behalf of the purchaser and, as a result, ease his or her suffering in purgatory.[179] The sale of indulgences was gradually eliminated after the sixteenth century. The Eastern Church does not believe in purgatory but, rather, continues to believe in an intermediate stage where souls pre-taste heaven and hell. In short, for the Eastern Orthodox Church there is "no repentance for humans after death."[180] It is significant to note that the Eastern Church never adopted or condoned the sale of indulgences.

---

[179] While beyond the scope of this work, issues surrounding the sale of indulgences are among the most fascinating in Christian church history. In essence, the Roman Catholic Church claimed it had the power to sell spiritual assets that would help souls successfully navigate through purgatory. But if purgatory was truly within the realm of the Church on earth, as the Roman Catholic Church claimed, couldn't indulgences be purchased for the dead as well? In 1476, Pope Sixtus IV in fact extended the applicability of indulgences to those already believed to be in purgatory. One need not stretch the imagination too far to arrive at resultant scenarios that question whether indulgences provided exemptions not only from the suffering resulting from sin, but also from the very culpability of sin. Could one purchase indulgences for sins not yet committed? So long as a loved one (or a will of an individual so directing) upon his or her death provided for the adequate purchase of indulgences, couldn't that individual knowingly live an exceptionally sinful life without worrying about the consequences of his or her earthly actions?

[180] Καρμίρη, σ. 59.

VI.   Other Differences

A. Fasting

Several councils of the early Church addressed the issue of fasting.[181] While the Eastern Orthodox Church continues to have more than 200 days of fasting during the calendar year for both its monastic and non-monastic faithful, the Roman Catholic Church significantly relaxed the days of required fasting at Vatican II.[182] It appears likely that the next Pan-Orthodox Council will establish less stringent rules for fasting for non-monastic Orthodox faithful.[183]

B. The Paschal Cycle

Disagreements arose in the early Church over the date of Easter. The First Ecumenical Council of 325 attempted to resolve these disagreements by arriving at a

---

[181] *See, e.g.*, Mastrantonis, *The Sacred Canons*, p. 33 (Regional Synod of Laodicea, canon 50, stating that "the whole of Lent should be kept by fasting on dry food.")

[182] Fasting for a brief period of time prior to receiving Holy Eucharist and fasting from meat on Fridays (after taking into consideration the age and health of the faithful) remain requirements of the Roman Catholic Church.

[183] Damaskenos, p. 29.

single method for determining the day Easter would be celebrated. Although no canon survives, we know from other sources that the Council determined that Easter is to be celebrated on the first Sunday after the first full moon following the spring equinox.[184] However, over the centuries, objections were voiced to Easter being celebrated with or before the Jewish Passover. Yielding to this pressure, the Byzantine jurist Ioannes Zonaras added a famous proviso to the original formula from 325 A.D., namely, the precondition that the Jewish Passover must occur before Easter.[185] The Roman Catholic Church does not take into account this proviso and, as a result, often celebrates Easter before or during the eight days of the Jewish Passover period. An equally important reason for the difference in Eastern and Western dates for Easter is that the East determines the spring equinox according to the Julian ("Old") calendar, while the West does so according to the more accurate Gregorian ("New") calendar.[186] Hence, even using the same formula would not guarantee that the two Churches arrive at the same Easter date determination.

---

[184] Patrinacos, pp. 125-26.

[185] Ibid., p. 126.

[186] Ibid., p. 127.

C. Canonization of Saints

The late Rev. George Mastrantonis in his pamphlet, *The State of Sainthood*, provides an overview of the important qualifications necessary for Eastern Orthodox sainthood:

> *The consideration and proclamation of a person as a saint of the church is made after his death by the people [first] of his local church. . . . He must have been a martyr of the Christian faith, or/and lived a pious and holy life, given extraordinary service to the church, or performed unanimously acknowledged miracles during his lifetime, and especially after death by intercession.*[187]

As is evident from the above, the proclamation of sainthood in the Eastern Orthodox Church depends largely on the consent of the people. Canonization is a rare occurrence in the Eastern Orthodox Church. One of the most-recently canonized saints in the Greek Orthodox Church is St. Nektarios, bishop of Pentapolis in Aegina, Greece, who was canonized in 1961. In contrast, the Roman Catholic Church canonizes its saints more

---

[187] Mastrantonis, *The State of Sainthood*, p. 7-8.

liberally. Through September 2002, Pope John Paul II alone had canonized 1,047 persons and beatified 475 persons during his papacy, an enormous amount even by Western standards.[188]

VII. Current Attempts at Reconciliation

An environment of rapprochement between the two Churches began in the 1960s, when the Second Vatican Council softened the Roman Catholic Church's position with respect to the Eastern Orthodox Church[189] and Pope Paul VI and Ecumenical Patriarch Athenagoras gathered in Jerusalem for an historic meeting, the first meeting of Pope and Ecumenical Patriarch since the Council of Florence in the fifteenth century. The simultaneous lifting of the anathemas on December 7, 1965 followed the

---

[188] Woodward, pp. 50-51. Among those Pope John Paul II beatified was Pope Pius IX (1846-78), a controversial personality of the nineteenth century who, among other things, convened Vatican I, which declared papal infallibility.

[189] For instance, Vatican II accepted the Eastern Orthodox sacraments and granted Roman Catholic faithful permission to partake in them, especially those of Confession, Eucharist and Unction. Abbott, p. 383-84, n. 54.   However, the Standing Conference of the Canonical Orthodox Bishops in America in its meeting of January 22, 1965, declared that "Eucharistic Mystery . . . is the end of unity, not the means to that end." Abbott, p. 385. Hence, Roman Catholic faithful currently are not permitted to receive Holy Eucharist in the Eastern Orthodox Church.

leaders' meeting and paved the way for intensive meetings to enable the two Churches to openly discuss and, eventually, reconcile their major differences. Since 1980, representatives of both Churches have met as a "Joint International Commission."[190] Also, the Bilateral Committee of Orthodox and Roman Catholic Theologians has been meeting for over thirty-five years in the United States. Its consultations have produced "agreed statements" on many issues, including the filioque in 2003.

The journey towards reconciliation has hit several bumps in the road. Most recently, the demise of Communism in Eastern Europe and the former Soviet Union resulted in concern about modern-day Uniatism (i.e., co-opting the churches to accept the primacy of the Pope but retain their distinct identity) and the confiscation of Eastern Orthodox Church properties.[191] This obstacle

---

[190] This Commission skirted the most troubling issues between the two Churches, but took positive steps towards reconciliation by issuing agreed statements on topics such as the sacraments and Apostolic Succession.

[191] The press widely reported the religious division between Eastern Orthodox and Roman Catholics in the Ukraine on the eve of a visit by the Pope. The Patriarch of Moscow lamented, "I find it difficult to be understanding when I see in this day and age Catholics oppressing three Orthodox dioceses in Ukraine, when people are driven out of their churches, when priests are attacked and the saints are the target of blasphemes." Tyler, p. A3.

has proved a formidable one, as demonstrated by the failure of the Joint International Commission to produce a joint statement on the subject in its eighth plenary session in Baltimore in the summer of 2004. And yet, the formal and informal bilateral consultations and discussions have continued.

The two central figures in recent reconciliation efforts have been Ecumenical Patriarch Bartholomeos I and the late Pope John Paul II. After the failure at Baltimore, the two leaders agreed that it was their duty to resume Orthodox-Catholic dialogue and, in 2004, the Ecumenical Patriarch traveled to Rome for a visit that the Pope described as a "leap ahead in the dialogue and the strengthening of fraternal relations." In his many travels, the dynamic Ecumenical Patriarch has steadfastly pursued a strengthening of the Eastern Orthodox Church's relations with other Churches and faiths (including his condemnation of those who mocked Islam in the "Comics Wars" of early 2006). Newly-elected Pope Benedict XVI appears equally determined, making ecumenism a priority of his pontificate.

A significant positive event in the relations between the two Churches in quite some time occurred during Pope John Paul II's March 2000 pilgrimage to

Jerusalem, where he asked for forgiveness for the Roman Catholic Church's conduct in prior centuries. Shortly thereafter, the Pope specifically asked forgiveness for the Roman Catholic Church's treatment of the Eastern Orthodox Church and its faithful during a meeting in Greece with Archbishop Christodoulos of Athens.[192] In fact, the Pope went so far as to refer to the Crusades, confessing the following:

> *It is tragic that the assailants, who had set out to secure free access for Christians to the Holy Land, turned against their own brothers in the faith. The fact that they were Latin Christians fills Catholics with deep regret. . . We entrust the heavy burden of the past to [God's] endless mercy, imploring Him to heal the wounds that still cause suffering in the spirit of the Greek people.[193]*

---

[192] In relevant part, the Pope stated the following: "For the occasions past and present, when the sons and daughters of the Catholic Church have sinned by actions and omissions against their Orthodox brothers and sisters, may the Lord grant us the forgiveness we beg of Him." *Pope Asks Forgiveness* 1.

[193] Howard.

[194] As Archbishop of Greece Christodoulos lamented, "Traumatic experiences remained as open wounds on [the Greek people's] vigorous body. . . Yet until now, there has not been heard even a single request for pardon." *Pope Asks Forgiveness* 1.

This was the first formal admission or expression of sorrow by the Roman Catholic Church for its conduct towards the Eastern Orthodox Church.[194] The Pope's sincere apology encouraged a peaceful co-existence and re-conciliation between the Churches, particularly for those who felt that Rome had remained indifferent to its treatment of Eastern Orthodox Christians, many of whom suffered profoundly for keeping the faith and traditions of the Lord and His Apostles.[195]

While teachings such as the filioque and the supremacy and infallibility of the Pope are deeply troubling to the East, the Roman Catholic Church remains among all other Christian denominations the nearest to the Eastern Orthodox Church. As manifested in each Divine Liturgy, the Eastern Orthodox Church prays that the Churches continue to re-examine the sources of their faith and Holy Tradition to find common ground upon which to build unity.[196]

---

[195] Pope John Paul II made other tremendous gestures to towards the Eastern Orthodox Church, including the return of the holy relics of St. John Chrysostom and St. Gregory the theologian to the Ecumenical Patriarchate in November 2004.

[196] "For the peace in the whole world, for the well-being of the Holy Churches of God, and for the union of all, let us pray to the Lord." Papadeas, p. 11.

PART THREE: DIFFERENCES WITH THE MAJOR PROTESTANT DENOMINATIONS

I. The Origins of Protestantism

The Roman Catholic Church suffered a period of turmoil following the Great Schism. Estranged from the original teachings of the early Church, it underwent dogmatic, traditional and liturgical changes which, in turn, contributed to the next trauma to the Christian faith—the Protestant Reformation, as the overall movement came to be known—whereby certain churches began splintering from the Roman Catholic Church and, ultimately, from one another.

For some, the primary cause of the rupture of the Roman Catholic Church was its stark abuse of power. J. Leslie Dunstan, a Protestant theologian, characterizes the state of the Roman Catholic Church at the time of the Protestant Reformation as follows:

> *The leaders of the Church, the papal court, and the clergy of every rank devoted themselves to their own interests with the result that in all too many cases selfishness,*

*love of luxury, nepotism, simony, and
immorality had become the marks of the
Church.[197]*

Against the backdrop of the humanitarian
awakening of the fifteenth and sixteenth centuries, these
conditions became unacceptable to certain western
European faithful who began to protest the Roman
Catholic Church's oppression and excesses. Among other
things, these faithful were disillusioned by the governance
of the Pope and by the sale of indulgences. Moreover,
they felt distanced by their Church's trampling of
individual rights and by the means it employed to obtain
obedience, including, in extreme cases, burning at the
stake those who had fallen into disfavor.

At first, the protestors pushed for reform within the
Roman Catholic Church. Yet, the Church remained
intractable. In fact, instead of addressing the early
concerns that caused the Protestant Reformation, the
Roman Catholic Church responded by elevating the Pope
to "Vicar of Christ" at the mid-sixteenth century Synod of
Trent. This effectively meant that the Pope alone
represented Christ in all earthly matters, thus further

---

[197] Ibid., p. 9-10.

70

advancing the Pope's primacy and consolidating his power. Suffice it to say that this was not a reaction that comforted disillusioned Roman Catholic faithful. Indeed, "[m]en were made doubly aware of the state of the Church by their very inability to bring about any reform."[198] Ignored by Rome, full-fledged rebellion ensued.

By the end of the fifteenth century, much of Europe was embroiled in controversy and war. This volatility facilitated the ability of various Protestant groups to provide a stable option for dissatisfied Roman Catholic faithful. At this time, the Eastern Orthodox Church was struggling for its very survival, having fought off the Ottoman invaders until Constantinople finally fell in 1453. Enslaved and isolated, it was unable to offer the reformers a viable alternative to Rome.

Many of the protestors were pious believers who desired greater religious freedom. Three of them succeeded in sparking particularly radical changes. Perhaps the best known of all early Protestants is Martin Luther (1483-1546). Luther was a German Roman Catholic monk who was troubled by many aspects of the Roman Catholic Church. Having spent three years in an

---

[198] Ibid, p. 10.

Augustinian monastery, he espoused the Augustinian teaching of "absolute destination" (i.e., that man is predestined by God to either hell or Paradise). However, it was Luther's concern with the sale of indulgences that appears to have motivated him the most. In particular, he protested with fervor the sale of indulgences intended to raise money for the reconstruction of Peter's Basilica in Rome. Finally, in the defining moment of the Protestant Reformation, on October 31, 1517, Luther posted on the doors of the Royal Church at Wittenberg his Ninety-five Theses. In doing so, Luther decried the primacy of the Pope, the celibacy of the priesthood, purgatory, the sale of indulgences and the harsh papal methods of securing blind obedience.[199] However, instead of returning to the teachings and practices of the early Church and the decisions of the ecumenical councils, Luther turned a blind eye toward tradition and relied solely upon Scripture.

For instance, Luther advanced the theory of "justification (i.e., salvation) by faith alone" as opposed to salvation through faith and good works, denounced certain teachings of the early Church, questioned the actual conversion of the plain gifts during the Holy Eucharist, and entirely abolished other sacraments such as

---

[199] Στεφανίδου, σ. 586-88.

Chrismation, Holy Unction, and Ordination. (In fact, Luther himself eventually married a former Roman Catholic nun in 1525.) Thus, in his attempt to correct the errors and excesses of the Roman Catholic Church, Luther destroyed many of the foundations of the early Church and removed aspects of mysticism from Church ceremonies. Luther eventually was excommunicated from the Roman Catholic Church and died in 1546.

At about the same time Luther posted his Ninety-five Theses on the Cathedral door, Ulrich Zwingle (1484-1531) began his own Protestant movement in Switzerland, ultimately going further astray from early Church teachings than Luther had by abolishing intercessions to Virgin Mary and the saints. Zwingle also frowned upon liturgical services, considering them "Jewish celebrations."[200] He abolished fasting and monastic life, and permitted clergy to marry. Moreover, he denounced "free will" and, like Luther, believed in salvation by faith alone. In his book, *Architelis*, he stated that on matters of faith the only authentic source was Scripture.[201] In fact, Zwingle's theology followed a simple principle: if something is not explicitly mentioned in Scripture, then it

---

[200] Στεφανίδου, σ. 599.
[201] Ibid.

is not valid and should not be believed or practiced; if something is explicitly mentioned in Scripture, then it should be adhered to absolutely. As a result, Zwingle came to be at odds with Luther regarding the nature of Holy Communion. Unlike Luther, Zwingle believed that the bread and wine used in Holy Communion merely *symbolized* the Body and Blood of Christ and that Christ was not actually present during the sacrament. In 1531, Zwingle fought personally against the papal armies in the Battle of Kappel, lost, and was killed. His body was treated with indignity and burned, and his ashes were scattered.[202]

The third significant reformer, John Calvin (1509-1564), was a French monk who was associated with one of the already-numerous Protestant sects. Like the Protestant leaders who came before him, Calvin rejected tradition and relied solely on Scripture.[203] Calvin imposed very

---

[202] Παπαγιανίδου, σ. 304.

[203] Note that certain Protestants sometimes refer to the Bible as "Sola Scriptura," or the only source of authority.

[204] Παπαγιαννίδιου, σ. 302.

[205] Κολιτσάρα, Οι Διαμαρτυρόμενοι, σ. 74-78. Calvinist teachings evolved somewhat and Calvin's followers have survived as Presbyterians.

strict, systematic rules on his followers to enforce his teaching on predestination.[204] Similar to Luther, the basis of his teachings was that each individual is predestined to eternal Heaven or eternal damnation before his or her birth. In essence, Calvin preached that man has no free will and that his actions have nothing to do with his salvation.[205]

II. Common Protestant Beliefs and their Differences with Eastern Orthodoxy

The Protestant Reformation brought such confusion to western Christianity that groups began splintering from one another at a rapid pace. As a result, the Protestant denominations currently number in the hundreds and there is no single official "Protestant" dogma. In fact, many of the smaller, less mainstream Protestant denominations have kept little from the early Church and do not even refer to themselves as "churches." Nevertheless, because the Protestant denominations derived from the Roman Catholic Church, many of them have retained some of the Roman Catholic teachings, such as the filioque. The summary of differences below is an attempt to generalize beliefs common to certain mainstream Protestant denominations (such as the Lutheran, Baptist, Presbyterian, Methodist and Evangelical churches) and to point out differences with the Eastern Orthodox Church.

A. Holy Tradition, the Bible and the Church

Holy Tradition is manifested in many forms: oral tradition (i.e., oral history of religious events); iconographic and hymnologic tradition (i.e., artistic renderings of religious individuals and events); and liturgical tradition (i.e., how the faith has been practiced). Most Protestants do not accept Holy Tradition outside of Scripture as relevant to the teachings of Christ and the Apostles as set forth in the Bible.[206] And yet, the entirety of Holy Tradition is integral to the faith; even the Lord occupied Himself with rejecting the false traditions of the Pharisees.[207] Paul affirms the importance of tradition, saying: "So then, brethren, stand firm and hold to the traditions which you were taught by us, either by word of mouth or by letter."[208]

In fact, the Gospels themselves indicate that, in addition to Scripture, other forms of tradition attesting to Christ's own life validly exist. For example, St. John

---

[206] Κολιτσάρα, Οι Διαμαρτυρόμενοι, σ. 96.

[207] Mark 7:9-13; Matt. 23:1-3.

[208] II Thes. 2:15; *see also* II Tim. 2:2; I Cor. 11:2.

[209] John 21:25; *see also* I Cor. 11:34

closes his Gospel with a thought-provoking statement: "But there are also many other things which Jesus did; were every one of them to be written, I suppose that the world itself could not contain the books that would be written."[209]

While Protestants generally reject the concept of non-Scriptural Holy Tradition, the New and Old Testaments that are so fundamental to Protestant worship actually presuppose its acceptance, as the books that comprise them were determined by the decisions of regional councils and identified in the writings of the Apostolic Fathers. Put simply, it was the early Church that collected the New and Old Testament books,[210] hence developing the very Scripture that is read by Eastern Orthodox, Roman Catholics and Protestants alike.[211]

Again, for many Protestants, Scripture serves as the sole source of religious guidance. Yet when the faithful translate Scripture individually, inconsistency and

---

[210] Indeed, the "Bible is not 'alone' - it belongs to the Church." O'Callaghan, p. 13.

[211] Note that the Eastern Orthodox Church accepts 49 books of the Old Testament as authentic, God-inspired and critical for salvation, whereas Protestants generally accept only the 39 "protocanonical" books. The ten books not accepted by most Protestants are called the "Deuterocanonical" books by the Eastern Orthodox Church.

confusion result. Indeed, such translations bring on "their own destruction,"[212] as they occur without guidance from the documents and traditions of the Apostolic Fathers or the decisions of the councils. As evidenced by the results of the Protestant Reformation, individual interpretation of Scripture without the guidance of Holy Tradition results in perpetual disagreement and fragmentation.

By contrast, "in the early Church, the doctrine, worship, and structure of the Church were so interwoven that one could not be separated from the others."[213] Indeed, the Eastern Orthodox Church is the Church of the New Testament, "the pillar and bulwark of the truth,"[214] as enriched by the practice of the Apostles and the Apostolic Fathers and animated by the Holy Spirit,[215] which dwells in the Church. The institution of the Church cannot be replaced with Scripture alone, for the Church is the body of Christ[216] of which we are members,[217] and "Christ is the Head of the church."[218] From the Eastern

---

[212] II Pet. 3:16.

[213] Carlton, p. 33.

[214] I Tim. 3:15.

[215] John 16:13.

[216] Col. 1:24.

[217] Eph. 5:30.

[218] Eph. 5:23.

Orthodox point of view, it is not possible for someone to translate and explain Scripture outside of the Church and without Holy Tradition.[219]

B. Free Will and Predestination

When Paul says, "For by grace you have been saved through faith,"[220] he means that God already gave us Divine Grace abundantly when He sent us His Only Begotten Son, Jesus Christ, to show us the way.[221] As discussed above, many Protestants have placed little or no emphasis on free will. In contrast, the Eastern Orthodox Church believes that man's choices on earth (or "faith working through love"[222]) and the gift of God (or Divine Grace channeled through the sacraments) guide him to salvation. Indeed, it is free will that enables man to resist evil.[223] As St. Cyril of Alexandria said, "from the origin

---

[219] Κολιτσάπα, Οι Διαμαρτυρόμενοι, σ. 96-97. By extension, there is no salvation outside the Church "because salvation *is* the church." Florovsky, p. 38 (emphasis added). In his third century *Extram Ecclesia Nula Salus*, St. Cyprian compares the Church with the Ark of Noah, saying: "If anyone could have been saved outside the ark of Noe, then he who is outside the church is saved." Danielou, p. 83.

[220] Eph. 2:8.

[221] Eph. 2:4-10.

[222] Gal. 5:6; James 2:17.

[223] Rom. 13:12. Note that "[t]he Church Fathers, especially of the Greek East, almost never used the term 'free will'. . . . Rather, they chose the term...'self-determination.'" Harakas, p. 223.

of creation man received control over his desires."[224] "Having been created with free will, man is allowed the privilege of facing the eternal consequence of either his 'yes' (heaven) or his 'no' (hell) to God."[225]

Many Protestants believe that man is predestined before birth to either Paradise or Hell and, therefore, that "the human basis for salvation is faith and faith alone," not good works.[226] This notion rejects the words of St. James that "faith apart from works is dead."[227] Just as the body without the spirit is dead, so faith without good works also is dead.[228]

In the Eastern Church there is no such thing as being saved by faith alone; rather, faith, good works and Divine Grace are all necessary for salvation. Salvation is a synergy of man and God, "[f]or He will render to every man according to his works."[229] The Eastern Church believes that the purpose of life is to use the power of the

---

[224] M.P.G. 69:24.

[225] Coniaris, *Introducing the Orthodox Church*, p. 122.

[226] Orr, p. 10. In the words of Luther, "a good man doeth good works." In other words, if a man is good, then he will naturally do good works.

[227] James 2:26.

[228] As Paul points out, "For we are . . . created in Christ Jesus for good works." Eph. 2:10.

[229] Rom. 2:6.

Holy Spirit to transform oneself as closely as possible into the likeness of God.[230] Hence, the best renewal and spiritual regeneration faithful can experience is when they worthily receive Holy Communion and thereby unite with Christ.[231] Indeed, a person is not fully saved until he is judged worthy and enters the Kingdom of God.[232]

C. The Sacraments

Although early Protestant denominations retained distorted versions of certain sacraments, most Protestant Churches today place little emphasis on sacramental mysticism. The Protestant notions of "my personal Savior, Jesus" and "justification by faith alone" disregard the role of the church as the mystical Body of Christ. In the words of Frank Schaeffer, the son of a Protestant preacher who discovered the Eastern Orthodox faith:

> *Protestants, since the beginning of the Reformation, have tended to reduce the way of salvation to a sort of magical one time, 'predestined' conversion experience . . . After all, if one can be instantly 'saved,' what need does one have of the spiritual tools . . . provided by a sacramental form of*

[230] II Cor. 3:18; O'Callaghan, p. 33.

[231] John 6:56.

[232] Matt. 12:36.

worship . . . ? Why not simply read John 3:16 once, 'believe,' and forget the rest of the Scripture?[233]

As we know from Scripture, the Church is an actual institution that was established by Christ and His Apostles. The Eastern Orthodox Church has continued the path of the Apostles and the early Church, believing that, indeed, "[t]he sacraments implement man's sanctification, uplifting his religious and moral life."[234]

1. Holy Eucharist

The Protestant Churches do not accept the Eastern Orthodox (and Roman Catholic) belief that during the Eucharist the plain gifts of bread and wine are changed by the Holy Spirit into the actual Body and Blood of Jesus Christ. Rather, "the Eucharist for them is a mere remembrance of the Last Supper."[235] Luther taught what came to be known as "consubstantiation"—that the Body and Blood are present *along with* the bread and wine. In other words, the gifts retain their own properties after consecration, even though they are united with the Body and Blood of Christ; hence, although the Lord becomes

---

[233] Schaeffer, p. 255.

[234] Mastrantonis, *A New Style of Catechism*, p. 111.

[235] Οικοδόμοι Πολιτισμού, σ. 294.

spiritually present through Holy Communion, He is not really present. Others, such as Zwingle, believed that the practice of partaking in Holy Communion was merely symbolic. In short, the change of the gifts does not exist for most Protestants; they disregard the statement in the New Testament attesting to Christ's intention, "He who eats my flesh and drinks my blood abides in me, and I in him."[236]

As previously discussed, for Eastern Orthodox faithful, Holy Communion is a bloodless sacrifice in spiritual form.[237] Indeed, the Holy Table is called the "Thysiasterion" (Θυσιαστήριον), or place of sacrifice.[238] The faithful offer the plain gifts and receive Holy Gifts, the very Blood and Body of the Risen Lord. In the Liturgy of St. Basil the Great, the gifts of bread and wine before consecration are called "antitypes" (αντίτυπα).[239] After the consecration, these antitypes become the mystical, spiritual Body and Blood of Jesus. St. Irenaeus wrote the following in his book, *Against All Heresies* (Κατά Πασών των Αιρέσεων): "the bread, which is

---

[236] John 6:56.

[237] "For Thou art the Offerer and the Offered, the accepted and the distributed, O Christ our God." Papadeas, p. 21.

[238] Vaporis, *The Divine Liturgy of St. Basil the Great*, p. 30.

[239] Ibid.

produced from the earth, when it receives the invocation of God, it is no longer common bread . . . [rather] it becomes the Eucharist, which is the Body and Blood of Christ." [240] Fr. Alexander Schmemann adds: "The Eucharist is the *parousia*, the presence and manifestation of Christ, who is 'the same to-day, yesterday and forever' (Heb. 13:8)."[241] Simply put, the presence of the Lord becomes real in Holy Communion.[242] Holy Communion

---

[240] Μωραΐτου, σ. 189; Richardson, p.388.

[241] *Introduction to Liturgical Theology*, p. 58.

[242] "Holy Communion provides man with the means and ability to be united with Christ. The branch bears fruit only while still remaining part of the vine." Dimopoulos, p. 154. St. Basil the Great in his Liturgy during the prayer after Consecration asks God the Father:

> *[U]nite us all to one another who become partakers of the one Bread and the Cup in the communion of the one Holy Spirit. Grant that none of us may partake of the holy Body and Blood of Your Christ to judgment or condemnation; but, that we may find mercy and grace with all the saints who through the ages have pleased You: forefathers, fathers, patriarchs, prophets, apostles, preachers, evangelists, martyrs, confessors, teachers, and every righteous spirit made perfect in faith. Especially for the most holy, pure, blessed, and glorious Lady, the Theotokos and ever virgin Mary.*

Vaporis, *The Divine Liturgy of St. Basil the Great*, p. 31. Hence, the Eucharist is a "transfiguration" for man. The sinful man can be both forgiven and transformed by the power of Holy Eucharist, becoming "God-like" (Θέωσις). In this way, all men can "become partakers of the divine nature." II Peter 1:4.

is thus the center and the climax of Orthodox worship. It is the "sacrament of sacraments."

Obviously, this view contrasts sharply with those of most Protestant denominations, even with those adhering to belief in consubstantiation. Saints and commentators have addressed the skepticism of Luther and those who came before him. For example, St. Cyril of Jerusalem asked rhetorically, "He once turned water into wine, in Cana of Galilee, at His own will, and is it incredible that He should have turned wine into blood?"[243] As St. John of Damascus stated, "And now you ask, 'How does the bread become Christ's Body, and the wine and water become Blood?' I tell you, the Holy Ghost comes and makes these Divine Mysteries . . . to be Christ's Body and Blood."[244]

2. Baptism

Some Protestant denominations administer baptism by immersion (though none of them by triple immersion), while others baptize by pouring or sprinkling water. More importantly, only a few of them administer baptism for the

---

[243] Cross, p. 68.

[244] Coniaris, *Introducing the Orthodox Church*, p. 136.

remission of sins.[245] In fact, for many Protestants, baptism is not considered a sacrament or a saving force but, rather, an external ceremony of membership. Moreover, although we know that Paul administered baptism to entire households,[246] some Protestant denominations do not administer baptism to infants but, instead, reserve it for adults who profess their faith.

3. Chrismation

Although we know that Chrismation was a sacrament in the early Church, most Protestants do not consider it a sacrament.   John Calvin, in particular, placed more of an emphasis on the proper catechism of children, and decried Confirmation (again, as Chrismation is generally known to Roman Catholocs and Protestants) as a "misborn wraith of a sacrament."[247] The Episcopal Church, however, generally performs Chrismation on

---

[245] Titus 3:5-6. In the Eastern Orthodox view, Baptism is performed both as a sacramental initiation into the Church, entitling the baptized to the other sacraments, as well as for the remission of sins. Indeed, as the priest says during the sacrament, "Having regenerated this Your servant by water and Spirit, granting remission of both voluntary and involuntary sins." Kezios, p. 32.

[246] Acts 16:15; I Cor.1:16.

[247] McNeill and Battles, 1460-61.

children aged twelve or older by the laying on of hands by the bishop.[248]

4. Repentance and Confession

Most Protestants do not believe that a priest is necessary for confession and repentance to occur.[249] They believe that they may, and do in fact, confess to one another. This is another unfortunate example of a Protestant reaction to the excesses of Rome resulting in the disregard of fundamental early Christian beliefs and practices. As discussed above, the Apostles were granted the ability to forgive and retain sins.[250] Through Apostolic Succession (discussed below), this ability has been passed to priests, who must give the proper instructions and read the appropriate prayers for forgiveness to a truly repentant person. Indeed, the Gospels tell us that canonically ordained clergy representing the Apostles are granted the right to forgive and retain sins.

5. Ordination

In the Eastern Orthodox Church, ordination of clergy is a sacrament. Candidates are ordained by the

---

[248] Χατζή Δημητρίου, σ. 74.

[249] James 5:16.

[250] John 20:23; Matt. 18:18.

87

laying on of hands by a bishop who, in turn, was ordained by two or three bishops, and so on, in an unbroken succession from the time of Christ and His Apostles. This is called "Apostolic Succession." Protestants do not have clergy that are canonically ordained in Apostolic Succession and by the laying on of hands by a bishop.[251]

Moreover, for many Protestants the clergy lacks a hierarchy of orders. (such as deacons and presbyters), and have done away with the concept of the bishop.[252] The early Christian Church could not comprehend a Church without a hierarchy of clergy and without bishops. St. Ignatius in his letter to the Smyrneans, written at the end of the first century, states:

> *Let no man do aught of things pertaining to the Church apart from the bishop. Let that be held a valid eucharist which is under the bishop or one to whom he shall have committed it. Wheresoever the bishop shall appear, there let the people be; even*

---

[251] I Tim. 4:14; II Tim. 1:6. Considering them Protestants for the moment, Anglicans (or, Episcopalians, as they are known in the United States) have insisted since the sixteenth century that their ordination has followed Apostolic Succession. However, while "Rome and the Orthodox agree that [Apostolic Succession] exists, [they] deny or doubt the Anglican claim to possess it." Hodges, p. 54 n.1.

[252] Note that Anglicans, if they may be considered Protestants, have kept all three orders (deacons, presbyters and bishops).

as where Jesus may be, there is the universal Church.[253]

In addition, most Protestant denominations permit the ordination of women, causing those Churches to drift further from the Eastern Church. The Eastern Orthodox Church believes that, from the early Church, men and women have performed different functions in Church life. "All human beings, and certainly all members of the Church, . . . are called to be 'temples of the Holy Spirit'... But not all are created and called to do so in the same way."[254] The early Church permitted women to occupy the office of "deaconess," for which there were limited functions.[255] However, "[t]he priesthood belongs to Christ and those ordained to perpetuate his priesthood are his icons."[256]

6. Holy Unction

With the exception of the Anglicans, if they can be regarded as Protestants to begin with, most Protestants

---

[253] Μωραΐτου, σ. 182 (citing Ignatius in his letter to the Smyrneans (8:1-2)); Richardson p. 115. "It is the Bishops of the Church who mark out the unity of the Church within its boundaries, by clarifying the faith of the Church, its discipline and its order." Harakas, p.175.

[254] Hopko, p. 169.

[255] One of these functions was to assist in the baptism of adult women. White, p. 199.

[256] Litsas, p. 50.

reject completely the sacrament of Holy Unction. Nevertheless, they pray for the sick and, in fact, are very involved in establishing and maintaining medical centers in the United States.

7. Marriage

Marriage in the Protestant churches typically consists of a simple ceremony absent the sacramental meaning of the Eastern Orthodox marriage ceremony,[257] which gives expression to basic truths about the most intimate of human relationships that God created and ordained, a "union of love."[258] The Eastern Orthodox Church permits and performs marriages between Protestants and Eastern Orthodox as an accommodation to the Eastern Orthodox party, as long as the Protestant party has been baptized in his/her Church in the name of the Holy Trinity (i.e., the Father, Son and Holy Spirit) and the couple promises to raise its children in the Eastern Orthodox Church. The Eastern Orthodox Church, however, will not recognize a marriage performed in a Protestant Church.

---

[257] Παπαγιαννίδου, σ. 313.
[258] Eph. 5:21-33.

D. External Influences on Mystical Worship

Many Protestant denominations have rejected early Church prayers, hymns and writings, instead placing an emphasis on the sermon. Moreover, the church structures themselves are oftentimes stripped of aesthetic physical beauty and are devoid of the ceremonial use of utensils and symbols.

Mystical worship has been called "the burning heart centered on God." The Eastern Orthodox Church believes that external influences, such as symbolic actions in worship and the interior aesthetics of the church, aid the believer in raising his heart and mind to heaven. Panagiotis Trempelas, a renowned Greek Orthodox theologian, quotes:

> *Someone can find in Orthodox worship a combination of human greatness and divine mystery. Someone can find in her the children's simplicity, philosophical depth, aesthetic satisfaction, and noble splendor, all analyzed in a magnificent rhythm of formal liturgical expression.*[259]

---

[259] Τρεμπέλα, σ. 42-43.

The monk Nestor, an early Ukrainian historian, recounts the beauty of the Eastern Orthodox liturgy, as reported by emissaries sent by Prince Vladimir of Kiev in 987 A.D. to find the best religion for his people. Among other places of worship, the emissaries entered the cathedral of St. Sophia in Constantinople. Their report described the following:

> *[T]he Greeks led us to the edifices where they worship their God, and we knew not whether we were in heaven or on earth. For on earth there is no such splendor or such beauty, and we are at a loss how to describe it. We only know that God dwells there among men, and their service is fairer than the ceremonies of other nations. For we cannot forget that beauty.*[260]

Indeed, during the Eastern Orthodox liturgy, all human senses are in action: we see, hear, smell, taste, and touch. The Holy Cross, the icons, the candles, the vestments, the utensils, the incense, and the music all help

---

[260] Taft, p. 112 (citing the Chronicle of Nestor); Στεφανίδου, pp. 407-08. Professor Robert Taft adds: "The Eastern Churches for the most part have remained faithful to the liturgical spirit of the golden age of the Fathers, when pagan society became christendom by the saving power of Word and Sacrament celebrated in the liturgical assembly. In a very real sense the whole life of the Church in the patristic period was 'liturgical.'" p. 112.

the faithful to transcend and participate in the service, hence acquiring a deeper understanding of the church's dogma and tradition. To this end, Eastern hymnology is particularly critical and unique.[261]

In contrast, and by way of example, most Protestant churches do not use incense (θυμίαμα) at all in their services. Ceremonial use of incense is not new to Christian worship. In fact, it was one of the precious gifts offered to the infant Christ upon his birth.[262] The burning of incense is a prayer offering of the people[263] and a practice that is expected of the faithful.[264] As stated in Psalm 141:2, we expect our prayers to be accepted by God and be pleasant to Him, just as the aromatic fumes of incense are pleasant to us.[265]

---

[261] "Byzantium's gift to the volume of world poetry is her hymnography . . . Always the ears of the sacred poets listened for and heard the celestial melodies of angels singing before the heavenly throne. The angels rather than Homer and Pindar provided models for the hymnographers. What the sacred poets heard, their pens brought down to earth, enabling the Church to sing in harmony with the angelic choirs." Eva Catafygiou Topping, *Byzantine Hymnology*, in Vaporis, *Three Byzantine Poets*, pp. 1-2.

[262] Matt. 2:11.

[263] Rev. 8:3-4.

[264] Mal. 1:11.

[265] Ps. 141:2. It is said that the smell of incense reminds the Devil of God's territory and warns him to stay out of holy places and, especially, out of a Christian's life. In tracing the development of the Christian use of incense, Gregory Dix identifies three types of use: (1) "domestic" or "fumigatory" use, (2) "honorific" use, and (3) use as a "sin-offering." Dix, p. 429.

Many Protestant churches today do, however, light candles in their altars and use candles with some symbolic meaning. In the Eastern Orthodox Church, candles and oil are provided as pure offerings of the faithful to the Lord, the Eternal Light and "light of the world."[266] Candles, especially those made of bee's wax, are considered the purest substance for a gift to the Lord. Virgin olive oil[267] is an offering with healing and sacramental powers and is used in Holy Unction,[268] Chrismation and in the "Everburning Light" on the Holy Table.

E. Calendar Issues

The Eastern Orthodox Church has inherited from the very early Church a weekly calendar cycle that designates certain days of the week in accordance with the events of Holy Week. For instance, each Sunday, we "come together and break bread and give thanks, first confessing [our] sins so that [our] sacrifice may be pure."[269] Also, we know that we "should fast on

---

[266] John 8:12.

[267] Olive oil is mentioned in several places in Scripture Ex. 27:20-21; Lev. 24:2.

[268] James 5:14-15.

[269] Richardson, p. 178; White, p. 56 (citing from Didache, or Teaching of the Apostles).

94

Wednesdays and Fridays" [270] in remembrance of the betrayal and the Crucifixion of the Lord. The Eastern Orthodox Church also follows the annual calendar, which chronicles the events of the life of Christ and commemorates the deaths of Virgin Mary, the martyrs and the saints of the church.[271] The saints are the church's heroes, "friends of God"[272] and examples of Christian life. Indeed, we find numerous invocations to the saints in catacombs where early Christians went to escape the persecution of open Christian worship. The Eastern Orthodox Church continues this tradition, believing that the saints are entitled to be honored and commemorated.[273]

---

[270] White, p. 57 (citing from Didache, or Teaching of the Apostles); Richarson, p. 174.

[271] Commemoration of a saint's death is really a celebration of the saint's "new" birth. It is interesting to note that Eastern Orthodox faithful traditionally place a greater emphasis on celebrating the holiday of the saint they are named after rather than their own birthdays. Similarly, Eastern Orthodox faithful place a greater emphasis on Easter rather than Christmas.

[272] Psalm 139:17 in Χαστούπη, σ. 207. Note that the reference to saints as "friends of God" is from the *Septuagint*, the original Greek translation of the Old Testament by "The Seventy" (i.e., the 72 learned individuals whom Ptolemy II, ruler of Alexandria, Egypt, from 285-46 B.C., appointed to translate the original biblical manuscripts for the benefit of the over one million Greek-speaking Jews within his jurisdiction) and, some say, at the behest of the head of the library of Alexandria. Μπρατσιώτου, σ. 280.

[273] Note again that the hymns and prayers to Virgin Mary and the saints are praises and intercessions only, for worship belongs only to the Holy Trinity.

Protestants generally have no annual calendar for holidays commemorating Virgin Mary, the martyrs and the saints.[274] In fact, as a reaction to the perceived excess of attention to Virgin Mary by the Roman Catholic Church, Protestants greatly decreased the emphasis on Virgin Mary, [275] rejecting the essential titles of "Mother of God," "Ever Virgin" and "the most blessed,"[276] and also largely cast aside the importance of the saints. Yet, there has been a newfound interest by Protestants in the importance of Virgin Mary.

---

[274] Παπαγιαννίδου, σ. 316.

[275] The fact that Virgin Mary has been so marginalized by the Protestant churches is perhaps most distressing to the Eastern Orthodox Church. After all, as Luke notes, she is "the mother of my Lord." Luke 1:43. And yet, most Protestant churches seldom mention her name during services or in sermons. As the Rev. Dr. Dumitru Macaila points out:

> Yes, His rejection goes on! Doesn't it mean to reject Christ if one rejects the one whose womb was 'broader than the heavens' since she contained the One Who cannot be contained, the One Who contains the whole universe? Doesn't it mean to reject Christ if one despises His dear mother, the one who made possible the Incarnation by cooperating with the will of God?

p. 12.

[276] Luke 1:28, 42. This latter name is one she was called by the Archangel at the Annunciation.

F. The Sign of the Cross and its Veneration

Protestants generally do not make the sign of the Cross. Also, although many Protestant denominations use the symbol of the cross inside and outside their churches, they do not venerate it. As previously discussed, making the sign of the Cross was a practice of the early Church that has been preserved by the Eastern Orthodox Church to remind us that Christ was crucified for our salvation. St. Cyril of Jerusalem in the fourth century affirms:

> *Let us not be ashamed to confess the crucified. Let the cross as our seal be boldly made with our fingers upon our brow, and on all occasions; over the bread we eat, over the cup we drink; in our comings and in our goings; before sleeping, when falling asleep and when arising; when walking, when resting. It is a powerful safeguard.*[277]

Paul adds, "far be it from me to glory except in the cross of our Lord Jesus Christ."[278] Veneration of the Holy Cross by the Eastern Orthodox faithful is a very important

---

[277] Catecheses (xiii, 36); M.P.G. 33,816.
[278] Gal. 6:14.

97

practice, for the Holy Cross is the supreme symbol of the greatest sacrifice and victory of the Lord for the human race.[279]

G. Memorial Services

We see many examples of prayers for the dead in the early Church, which believed—as the Eastern Orthodox Church continues to believe—that there is a communion between the church militant on earth and the church triumphant in heaven. Indeed, if we have prayers for the living, why not for the departed?[280] Eastern Orthodox faithful believe that the dead are concerned about us,[281] just as we are concerned about their place in heaven. Unlike the Eastern Orthodox Church, most Protestant Churches do not have memorial services or prayers for the dead during Sunday services, although some may have special memorial services and prayers.

---

[279] Gal. 6:14; Col. 2:14-15; I Cor.1:18.

[280] II Mac. 12:40-45. "The prayer of a righteous man has great power in its effects." James 5:16.

[281] John 8:56; Luke 16:19-31.

H. Missions vs. Proselytism

Many Protestant Churches have organized foreign missionary programs in many parts of the world, often trying to gain converts out of Christians who are active members of another church. The Eastern Orthodox Church believes that this method of gaining members, called "proselytism," runs contrary to Christ's teachings and is of grave concern. "A real missionary is one who goes 'where the gospel has not yet been preached or is not being truly lived.'"[282]

---

[282] Shilling, p. 243 (quoting theologian Nikos A. Nissiotis from "Interpreting Orthodoxy," *The Ecumenical Review*, XIV (1961-62), p. 23).

EPILOGUE

About two years ago, Father Constantine Mathews honored me with the privilege of reviewing his manuscript comparing the dogmatic teachings of Orthodox, Catholic and Protestant Churches. I reviewed his manuscript and kept it for an unduly long time, reading it over again and again. As a professor of dogmatic theology, indeed, this was a labor of love.

The difficulty of the task at hand demonstrates the author's dedication and love for the Church. It is easy for theologians to be strict and inflexible in theory, and conciliatory in action. Father Mathews' work is of relevance and importance to theologian and layman alike, especially to those who teach. The book's vast reservoir of analysis is manna for those desiring to know more about our faith and the vast differences amongst our brethren.

EXHIBIT A
THE HOLY TRINITY AND
FILIOQUE

THE EASTERN ORTHODOX TEACHING OF THE HOLY TRINITY
The first two Ecumenical Councils (A' at Nicea in 325 A.D. and B' at Constantinople in 381 A.D.) decreed that, based on John 15:26 and Acts 2:33, the Hierachical Order of the Holy Trinity is as follows:

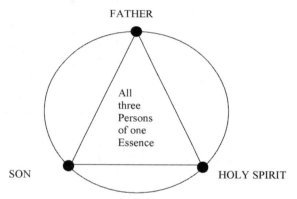

THE ROMAN CATHOLIC FILIOQUE
The Roman Catholic Church added the concept that the Holy Spirit derives from the Father *and* from the Son.

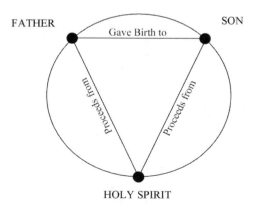

EXHIBIT B
A TIMELINE OF
CHURCH HISTORY

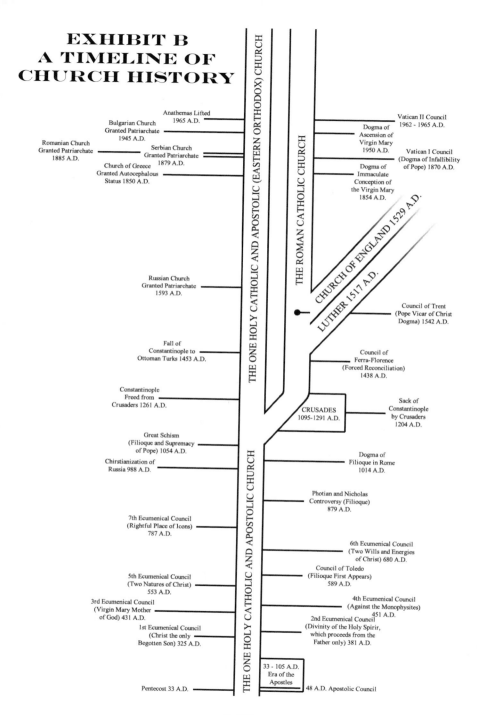

THE ONE HOLY CATHOLIC AND APOSTOLIC (EASTERN ORTHODOX) CHURCH

THE ROMAN CATHOLIC CHURCH

THE ONE HOLY CATHOLIC AND APOSTOLIC CHURCH

Anathemas Lifted
1965 A.D.

Bulgarian Church
Granted Patriarchate
1945 A.D.

Romanian Church
Granted Patriarchate
1885 A.D.

Serbian Church
Granted Patriarchate
1879 A.D.

Church of Greece
Granted Autocephalous
Status 1850 A.D.

Vatican II Council
1962 - 1965 A.D.

Dogma of
Ascension of
Virgin Mary
1950 A.D.

Vatican I Council
(Dogma of Infallibility
of Pope) 1870 A.D.

Dogma of
Immaculate
Conception of
the Virgin Mary
1854 A.D.

CHURCH OF ENGLAND 1529 A.D.

LUTHER 1517 A.D.

Russian Church
Granted Patriarchate
1593 A.D.

Council of Trent
(Pope Vicar of Christ
Dogma) 1542 A.D.

Fall of
Constantinople to
Ottoman Turks 1453 A.D.

Council of
Ferra-Florence
(Forced Reconciliation)
1438 A.D.

Constantinople
Freed from
Crusaders 1261 A.D.

CRUSADES
1095-1291 A.D.

Sack of
Constantinople
by Crusaders
1204 A.D.

Great Schism
(Filioque and Supremacy
of Pope) 1054 A.D.

Dogma of
Filioque in Rome
1014 A.D.

Chirstianization of
Russia 988 A.D.

Photian and Nicholas
Controversy (Filioque)
879 A.D.

7th Ecumenical Council
(Rightful Place of Icons)
787 A.D.

6th Ecumenical Council
(Two Wills and Energies
of Christ) 680 A.D.

Council of Toledo
(Filioque First Appears)
589 A.D.

5th Ecumenical Council
(Two Natures of Christ)
553 A.D.

3rd Ecumenical Council
(Virgin Mary Mother
of God) 431 A.D.

4th Ecumenical Council
(Against the Monophysites)
451 A.D.

2nd Ecumenical Council
(Divinity of the Holy Spirir,
which proceeds from the
Father only) 381 A.D.

1st Ecumenical Council
(Christ the only
Begotten Son) 325 A.D.

33 - 105 A.D.
Era of the
Apostles

Pentecost 33 A.D.

48 A.D. Apostolic Council

Father Mathews deserves admiration, praise and respect for his countless hours of work to master this most complex of subjects. The book leaves the reader inspired and appreciative of our treasure trove of Orthodoxy. May Father Mathews' shining example serve as a beacon for younger priests and theologians to emulate.

Father George Dimopoulos

Feast Day of Saint

Athanasios, 2004

BIBLIOGRAPHY

English Sources

Abbott, Walter M. *The Documents of Vatican II*. N.p.:
    American Press, 1966.
"Baptism and 'Sacramental Economy.'" An Agreed
    Statement of The North American Orthodox-
    Catholic Theological Consultation, St. Vladimir's
    Orthodox Seminary, Crestwood, New York, June 3,
    1999 ("Baptism Agreed Statement").
Calvin, John. *The Institutes of the Christian Religion*. John
    T. McNeill, ed. Ford Lewis Battles, trans. 2 vols.
    Philadelphia: Westminster Press, 1960.
Carlton, Clark. *The Way*. Salisbury: Regina, 1997.
Catechism of the Catholic Church. United States Catholic
    Conference, Inc.—Libreria Editrice Vaticana, (Eng.
    trans.) 1994.
Coniaris, Anthony M. *Introducing the Orthodox Church*.
    Minneapolis, MN:, 1982.
Coniaris, Anthony M. *These Are the Sacraments*.
    Minneapolis, MN: Light and Life, 1981.
Constantelos, Rev. Demetrios. "Background and Purpose
    of Orthodox Christian Iconography." *Orthodox
    Observer*, July 1997.
Cross, Frank Leslie, ed. *St. Cyril of Jerusalem's Lectures
    on the Christian Sacraments: the Protocatechesis
    and the Five Mystagogical Catecheses*. London:
    S.P.C.K., 1966.
Damaskenos, Metropolitan of Tranoupolis. *Towards the
    Great Council*. Chambesy, Geneva: S.P.C.K., 1972.

104

Daniellou, Jean. *The Bible and the Liturgy*. Notre Dame, IN: University of Notre Dame Press, 1966.

Dimopoulos, Rev. George, *Analysis of Forty Sermons from the Homilies of St. John Chrysostomos*. Margate City, NJ: West End Press, 2002.

Dix, Gregory. *The Shape of the Liturgy*. London: Dacre Press, 1975.

Dunstan, J. Leslie. *Protestantism*. New York: Washington Square Press, Inc., 1962.

Easton, Burton Scott. *The Apostolic Tradition of Hippolytus*. N.p.: Cambridge University Press, 1962.

"The Filioque: A Church-Dividing Issue?" An Agreed Statement of the North American Orthodox-Catholic Theological Consultation, Paul's College, Washington, D.C., October 25, 2003 ("Filioque Agreed Statement").

Florovsky, Georges, *Bible, Church, Tradition: An Eastern Orthodox View*. Vol. I. Belmont, MA: Nordland Publishing Company, 1972.

Frangopoulos, Athanasios S. *Our Orthodox Christian Faith*. Athens: Brotherhood of theologians, "O Sotir", 1993.

Harakas, Stanley Samuel. *Orthodox Christian Beliefs*. Minneapolis, MN: Light & Life Publishing Company, 2002.

Hallick, Mary Paloumpis. *The Story of Icons*. Brookline, MA: Holy Cross Orthodox Press, 2001.

Hodges, H. A. *Anglicanism and Orthodoxy*. London: SCM Press Ltd., 1957.

Hopko, Thomas. "On the Male Character of Christian
Priesthood." *St. Vladimir's Theological Quarterly*
19, (1975).

Howard, Michael. "Penitent Pope attempts to end holy
war." *The Guaradian*, May 5, 2001.

Ignatius, Saint of Antioch. *Letter to Philadelphians*,
Chapter 4, and *Letter to Smyrneans*.

Kalokyris, Constantine. *Orthodox Iconography*. Brookline,
MA: Holy Cross Orthodox Press, 1965.

Keifer, Ralf A. *Summary on Notes on Eucharistic Origins*.
Notre Dame, IN: n.p., 1975.

Kezios, Rev. Spencer T., ed. *Sacraments and Services,
Book I*. Northridge, CA: Narthex Press, 1995.

Knapp, Julie. "Images From the Past: Our Icons in the
Orthodox Church." *Theosis*, October 1982.

Kokkinakis, Bishop Athenagoras. *Christian Orthodoxy
and Roman Catholicism*. Boston: Greek Orthodox
Archdiocese of North and South America, National
Youth Office, 1956.

Litsas, Fotios, *A Companion to the Greek Orthodox
Church*. New York: n.p., 1984.

Lucker, Raymond A., Patric J. Brennan, and Michael
Leach, eds. *The People's Catechism*. New York:
Crossroad, 1995.

Macaila, Rev. Dr. Dumitru. "A World Rejecting God's
Truth?" *The Hellenic Voice*, August 7, 2002.

Mastrantonis, Rev. George. *Ancient Epitome of the Sacred
Canons of the Eastern Orthodox Church*. St. Louis,
MO: Logos Mission, n.d. (*"The Sacred Canons"*)

Mastrantonis, Rev. George. *A New Style Catechism*. St.
Louis, MO: Logos Mission, 1969.

Mastrantonis, Rev. George. *The State of Sainthood*. St. Louis, MO: Logos Mission, n.d.

Mastrantonis, Rev. George. *What is the Eastern Orthodox Church?* St. Louis, MO: Logos Mission, 1956.

Mastroyiannopoulos, Elias. *Nostalgia for Orthodoxy*. Athens: Zoe, 1959.

Mathews, Rev. Constantine. "The Last Supper and the Leavened Bread." *Orthodox Observer*, April 7, 1982.

Meyendorff, John. *Orthodoxy and Catholicity*. New York: Sheed & Ward, 1966.

Meyendorff, John. *Rome, Constantinople, Moscow*. N.p.: St. Vladimir's Seminary Press, 1966.

Migne, J.P., ed. *Patrologiae Cursus Completus; Series Latinae*. 221 vols. Paris, 1844-55 ("M.P.L.").

Mould, Daphne D.C. Pochin. *The Orthodox Church*. Chicago: Claretian Publications, 1972.

O'Callaghan, Paul. *An Eastern Orthodox Response to Evangelical Claims*. Minneapolis, MN: Light and Life P.C., 1984.

Orr, William W. *Ten Reasons Why I Believe the Bible is the Word of God*. Wheaton, IL: Scripture Press, n.d.

Papadeas, Fr. George, ed. and trans. *The Divine Liturgy of St. John Chrysostom*. Daytona Beach, FL: Patmos Press, 1988.

Patrinacos, Rev. Nicon D. *A Dictionary of Greek Orthodoxy*. New York, NY: Greek Orthodox Archdiocese of North & South America (Department of Education), 1984.

"Pope visits Greece; Asks Forgiveness for Sins Against Orthodox Christians." *The Hellenic Voice*, May 16, 2001.

Pulcini, Fr. Theodore. *Orthodoxy and Catholicism: What Are the Differences?* Ben Lomond, CA: Conciliar Press, 1995.

Putz, Louis I., C.S.C. *Vatican II, Its Problems and Gains*, Religion in Life. Notre Dame, IN: Abingdon Press, 1969.

Richardson, Cyril C. *Early Christian Fathers*, New York: The Macmillian Company, 1970.

Sacramentary, The. New York: Catholic Book Publishing Co., 1985.

Schaeffer, Frank. *Dancing Alone.* Brookline, MA: Holy Cross Press, 1994.

Schilling, S. Paul. *Contemporary Continental Theologians.* Nashville-New York: Abington Press, 1966.

Schmemann, Rev. Alexander. *The Eucharist.* Crestwood, NY: St. Vladimirs Seminary Press, 1987.

Schmemann, Rev. Alexander. *Introduction to Liturgical Theology.* Asheleigh E. Moorhouse, trans. London: The Faith Press Ltd., 1966.

Stephanou, Rev. Archimandrite Eusebius. *How the Orthodox Church Differs from Roman Catholicism.* Destin, FL: St. Symeon the New Theologian Orthodox Renewal Center, 1996.

Taft, Robert, SJ. *Beyond East and West.* Washington, DC: The Pastoral Press, 1984.

Tyler, Patrick E. "A Divided Ukraine Awaits the Pope." *New York Times*, June 23, 2001.

Vaporis, Fr. Nomikos M., ed. and trans. *The Divine Liturgy of St. Basil the Great.* Brookline, MA: Holy Cross Orthodox Press, 1988.

Vaporis, Fr. Nomikos M., ed. *Three Byzantine Sacred Poets.* Brookline, MA: Hellenic College Press, 1979.

Ware, Bishop Kallistos. *The Orthodox Way*. Crestwood, NY: St. Vladimir's Seminary Press, 2001.
Whalen, William J. *The Episcopalians*. Chicago: Claretian Publications, n.d.
White, James F. *Introduction to Christian Worship*. Nashville, TN: Abingdon Press, 1990.
Woodward, Kenneth L. "When Saints Go Marching In." *Newsweek Magazine*, September 4, 2000.
Zizioulias, Metropolitan John of Pergamon. "The Eucharist and the Kingdom (Part III)." *Sourozh: A Journal of Orthodox Life and Thought*, Vol. 60, May 1995.

Greek Sources*

Θεοδώρου, Ανδρέου. *Transubstantiatio-Concomitantia* καί Αποχή των Λαικών εκ του Αγίου Ποτηρίου. Αθήναι: n.p.,1967.
Καλλινίκου, Κωνσταντίνου, Ο Χριστιανικός Ναός καί τα Τελούμενα εν αυτώ. Αθήναι: Γρηγόρη, 1969.
Καλογήρου, Ιωάννου. Ορθόδοξος Θεώρησις της Β' Συνόδου του Βατικανού. Αθήναι: Παλαμιδάκη, 1967.
Καρμίρη, Ιωάννου. Η Δογματική Διδασκαλία του Ιωάννου του Δαμασκηνού. Αθήναι: n.p., 1940.
Καντιώτου, Αυγουστίνου Ν. (Μητροπολίτου Φλωρίνης). Κοσμάς ο Αιτωλός. Αθήναι: n.p., 1966.
Κολιτσάρα, Ιωάννου. Η Καινή Διαθήκη: Κείμενο καί Ερμηνευτική Απόδοσις. Αθήναι: Ζωή, 1981.

Κολιτσαρα, Ιωάννου. Η Δυτική Εκκλησία. Αθήναι: Ζωή, 1960.

Κολιτσάρα, Ιωάννου. Οι Διαμαρτυρόμενοι. Αθήναι: Ζωή, 1975.

Migne, J.P., ed. *Patrologiae Cursus Completus; Series Graeca.* 161 vols. Paris, 1857-66 ("M.P.G.").

Μπρατσιώτου, Παναγίωτου Ι. Επίτομος Εισαγωγή εις την Παλαιάν Διαθήκην. Αθήαι: Π. Συνοδινού, 1955.

Μωραΐτου, Δημητρίου. Ιστορία της Χριστιανικής Λατρείας. Αθήναι: Επιστημονική Επετηπίς, 1964.

Οικοδόμοι Πολιτισμού. Αθήναι: Αποστολική Διακονία, 1968.

Παπαγιαννίδου, Ευτυχίου. Η Νίκη και ο Θρίαμβος της Ορθοδοξίας απο του Σχίσματος μέχρι των καθ ημάς χρόνων. Τόμος Β'. Αθήναι: n.p., 1970.

Παπαδοπούλου, Χρυσοστόμου. Το Πρωτείον του Επισκόπου Ρώμης. Εκκλησία, 1964.

Στεφανίδου, Βασιλείου. Εκκλησιαστική Ιστορία. Αθήναι: Αστήρ, 1959.

Τρεμπέλα, Παναγιώτου. Η Ρωμαϊκή Λειτουργική Κίνησις και η Πράξις της Ανατολής. Εκκλησία, 1949.

Χαστούπη, Αθανασίου Π. Η Αγία Γραφή (Παλαιά Διαθήκη) Μετάφρασις των Εβδομήκοντα-Μετάφρασις Διωρθωμένου Εβρα κού Κειμένου. Τόμος Β'. Αθήναι: Αθηνα καί Εκδόσεις "Αθ. Φιλιόπουλος & Σία.," 1960.

Χατξή Δημητρίου, Οικ. Κώστα. Μεγάλη Ορθόδοξος Χριστιανική Κατήχησις. Σικάγο: n.p., 1929.

* These sources originally published in Greek have been translated, in relevant part, by Rev. Fr. Constantine Mathews for use in this work.